The Backward Person's Guide to Music

THE BACKWARD PERSON'S GUIDE TO MUSIC

Pause and think before you lash out four, or even five, pounds on a brand new Stradivarius—are you sure your chin is the right shape for the violin? If you live in a tenth-storey attic and you wish to take up the organ, are you positive you are doing the right thing?

This book contains information and advice about music that, it can safely be said, the reader will find nowhere else. How many people, for instance, know that the correct definition of Harmony is 'a discordant type of singing heard outside public houses'?

Mr. Rush leaves no note unturned in his ruthless exposé of music and musicians from the Stone Age to the Rock Age.

Mr. Holgate's illustrations show only too clearly how even if music hath charms, its exponents usually haven't.

The Backward Person's Guide to Music

by

Len Rush

with drawings

by

BEN HOLGATE

CRESCENDO PUBLISHING COMPANY

Boston

Standard Book Number 87597-023-0
Library of Congress Number 69-19316
Printed in Great Britain
for
Crescendo Publishing Co., Boston
by arrangement with Elek Books, Ltd.

Reprinted 1970

Contents

1

How Music Grew

MAN PROBABLY started to make music as far back as the Palaeolithic era. And that was a long time ago, before even the days of steam radio. It's more than likely that he first felt the urge while having his bath, though he didn't actually *sing*, of course (he couldn't even talk yet, the boob). But he could make some jolly interesting noises by slapping his chest, which he did fairly often on account of the cold and some of the crawly things that were left over from the primeval slime.

Man's Urge To Make Music

At that time a musically-minded person would be easily recognized from the colour of his body—i.e., black and blue. Eventually (when he'd had enough of the business of "suffering for one's art") he must have tried slapping other people's chests for a change. And this was a bit chancy as there were philistines even in those days. This unsatisfactory state of affairs existed until man suddenly got inhibitions and started wearing the odd garment; which had the effect of being good for his rheumatics but bad for his acoustics. Slapping, somehow, wasn't the same.

And To Share It

First Instrument

Ironically enough, it was the very skins he wore that went to make the first instrument, the drum. All the drummers in primitive times were women (in modern times all drummers are primitive men). This was because the drum was more of a tailoring job than anything else, and all the patching and so on was strictly *her* department. While his wife was beating out lullabies, man started making himself a rattle, and he filled it with things like pebbles and a few teeth that happened to be lying on the mantelpiece. He reckoned it was for the baby, but the baby never got a look in; it was little-Willie's-train-set business all over again. It was a long time before he found an instrument that satisfied him, however. He kept experimenting with things like bull-roarers, scrapers, and shells with holes in. You can imagine the noise that went on in the evenings, with father making all kinds of squeaks and groans and mother tapping away endlessly at her drum. Palaeolithic children must have had a rough time of it; no wonder they grew up anti-social.

Palaeolithic children must have had a rough time of it

The Egyptians' Idea Of Music

The Egyptians claimed that they invented all kinds of instruments, including lyres, flutes, and clarinets, but you can take that with a pinch of salt. It's true they used to carry things round with them which looked very arty and impressive, but if you examine their painting very carefully you'll see that their lyres have no strings and their flutes have no holes in them. One way and another, everything points to the fact that the Egyptians didn't add much to the art of music, long hair or not. But their orchestral concerts must have been lovely and quiet.

Music v. Greek Literature

The lyres used by the Greeks *did* have strings on them, though a good many well-known citizens wished they didn't. Plato was always giving musicians the rough edge of his tongue, and one can only assume that he was afraid that the new art would stop people reading books and throw him out of a job. Homer thought quite differently, and if you took all the passages concerning lyres away from the Iliad it would be a much shorter book.

Origin Of The Pan Pipes

The most popular instruments in Greek times, however, were the pan-pipes; and the origin of these was so unusual that you'd hardly credit it. It seems that one hot August afternoon a certain Arcadian nymph was cutting through the woods on the way back from her aunt's, when Pan happened to see her. It was a case of love at first sight, and he began to pursue her with a glint in his eye. The girl was no mean sprinter, and she held her own nicely, till she suddenly found herself trapped by the River Ladon. Now she'd heard all about the Fate Worse Than Death so she went over to a crowd of nymphs from a works outing party who happened to be paddling at the time. "I'm sorry to bother you", she said politely, "but would you mind turning me into a bundle of reeds? It's rather important." In those days this was just a run-of-the-mill request, and the girls duly obliged. When he saw that he'd been foiled again, Pan draped the reeds around his neck and wore them that way ever after. Whenever he felt melancholy he would breathe down them, and the nymph must have wondered if this *was* a Fate Worse Than Death, because Pan was a terror for garlic. For some unaccountable reason intellectuals like Plato were sceptical of this story—they said it wouldn't hold water. Consequently there was a kind of snobbish prejudice against pan-pipes, and they were strictly a working-class instrument. They were mostly played by shepherds during the lunch-hour, and by referees at the Olympic Games.

Birth Of The Orchestra

It was these same Greeks, of course, who invented the orchestra (not to mention the chorus). What happened was that they went and designed these enormous amphitheatres and then found they'd inadvertently left a large space in between the front row of the stalls and the stage. They were at a loss as to what to do with it, till someone hit on the idea of filling it with musicians. The orchestra turned out to be a boon to the Greek comedian, who often got a cheap laugh by making cracks at the players. When his script wasn't going over so well (Monday nights were always the worst) he would stroll over to the edge of the stage and call down to the conductor . . .

"Well, if it isn't my old friend Horace! Oh, I *say* Horace, I do like the whistle-and-flute—my word—real cloth, too!" (Winking at audience.) "By the way, people, you should have seen the suit Horace got married in—ee, I'll never forget it . . ."

In this way he leaned on Horace practically all the way through his act, finishing up with a little song about blue-birds over the old Aegean. Funnily enough, comedians have used this same technique ever since. And conductors still seemed to be called Horace.

The Romans took over a lot of things from the Greeks, but they didn't bother much with pan-pipes, which had unsavoury associations with peace and culture. Instead they invented their own instruments, such as the cornu and the tuba. Various Roman authors, whose names we won't go into (as a matter of fact, I can't spell them) referred to the noise made by the tuba as "raucus", "terribilis" and "horribilis". Now this is very significant, in that it came from gentlemen who spent their Saturday afternoons in amphitheatres watching people being torn to bits by lions, and shouting "encore". Those boys were no cissies, and if they said a thing sounded "horribilis" you can bet your boots it *was* "horribilis". And that is why the Romans decreed that these instruments should only be played (1) At funerals, or (2) During battles. In other words, practically all the time.

Romans' Determination To Keep Music In Its Place

Historians have always tended to neglect the important part played by Roman trumpets in helping the armies to build up the empire. The musicians were always sent in with the vanguard, and the effect was dramatic, to say the least. The noise used to drive Gauls, Germans and Britons crazy—which, as Caesar well knew, was half the battle. Even the Picts and Scots admitted that it fairly set their teeth on edge—and they'd been weaned on the bagpipes, mark you. The snag was, the wind had to be in the right direction for the Romans otherwise the noise would blow back on to their own men and drive *them* crazy. No wonder the standard-bearers played safe and always kept their ears covered.

Effect Of Roman Music On Barbarians

It isn't surprising that in times of peace most people preferred instruments like the lyre, which only had a few strings and couldn't really do a great deal of harm. They were ideal for singing with, and they were always carried around by the *troubadours*. These were professional and semi-professional singers who wandered round Europe in the early Middle Ages. They mostly consisted of aristocrats who were down on their uppers and thought that this mode of living was preferable to going into politics. As for taking people

Troubadours

round their castles for half-a-crown a nob—they thought that kind of thing was degrading in the extreme.

Function Of Domestic Troubadour

Every self-respecting middle-class family had its own troubadour, who had to play soothing music for the man of the house when he came home from business, help the children with their Latin homework, organize Christmas parties, and do a few odd jobs around the garden. His main function seemed to consist of amusing the boss's wife, while *he* was away at week-ends (this was the boss's idea, incidentally). The troubadours, many of whom had foreign blood in them, used to take these instructions far too literally; and often enough the husband would come back on Monday to an empty house, with milk still on the step and the fire out.

Some Names He Was Known By

Troubadours were more familiarly known in England as "minstrels", in parts of France they were "trouvères"; in Germany they were called "minnesingers" and in the law-courts they were known as "co-respondents".

Arrival Of The Lute

Vocal music was very popular right up to Elizabethan times, and it was then accompanied by the lute—an instrument that was brought into the country by merchant seamen, who found it was all the rage on the continent. Lots of songs of that time had a mournful sound to them, and usually ended on a painful, wobbling note. This was because of the way the lute was built; the bulging-out part used to stick in your tummy. The stouter serenaders gave it up as a bad job, and took up the virginal, named after the queen. All the songs of that period are very easy to identify because they had one thing in common: they all began with "O" . . . e.g., "O Mistress Mine", "O Would Thy Gaze Were Half As Strait", "O Sole Mio", etc. No doubt you can think of a lot more.

How The Orchestra Hadn't Progressed

For some reason, orchestras hadn't improved very much. They were now called "consorts", which has a ring of nastiness about it somehow. They usually were made up of strings, like lutes and viols, but occasionally when they had to play in some big dance-hall it was necessary to augment the group by adding a wind-instrument. When this happened, it was said in the profession that the band was now a "*broken* consort", which seems a bit hard on the chap who was good enough to help them out on the flute, or whatever it was. Playing a wind instrument about this time must have been a thankless job.

Classical Music For The Masses

Gradually music got around to the man-in-the-street, thanks to the efforts of the "classical" composers—that is to say, composers who catered for all classes. Handel, for example, had a live-wire of an agent named Heidigger (or Gold-digger, as he was affectionately known in Charing Cross Road) who got up to all kinds of tricks to bring music to the millions. It was he who persuaded Handel to write a special suite for Guy Fawkes Night, and another for the L.C.C. Water Board. He thought of absolutely everything. Incidentally, Handel was the first man for a very long time to write a piece specifically for the blacksmith's anvil. His idea was to encourage smithies to form their own anvil orchestras, but it never amounted to anything. Someone once wrote a poem about the village smithy's "iron bands", but no one seems to know where they played. The trouble was, no two anvils were of the same pitch, and they were fairly hard things to tune. You just didn't know where to start.

Music Comes Into The Home

Others, like Mozart and Haydn, joined in the play-it-yourself movement. They appreciated that the chances of the ordinary chap being able to get up an amateur symphony orchestra were fairly remote. And even if he succeeded there were all kinds of snags about getting seventy or eighty players into the front parlour (the piano would have to come out for a start, then it would have meant the host's wife laying on seventy-odd cups of tea, some with, some without, with literally *hundreds* of salmon-paste sandwiches). Well, Mozart and Haydn and a few more realized the position, and they started writing "chamber-music". There were "trios" for bachelor flats, "quartets" for council-houses, "quintets" for semi-detacheds, and so on. Bach went even further, and brought out a tune that you could perform in the larder if you felt so inclined (he was a great one for sticking up for the rights of minorities). It's still a bit of a mystery why he called this piece the "Air on a G String", because, so far as is known, G strings weren't worn by the ladies of that period. But then, the mind of genius is often years ahead of its time. Anyway, this work was a boon to all those with one-stringed fiddles made out of cigar-boxes, who looked on it as a sort of symbol of musical emancipation. Oddly enough, Bach didn't have a one-stringed fiddle himself. He didn't even smoke cigars.

The Romantic Composers

That was your classical composer then—hard-working, practical and abstemious (just the odd glass of Madeira at Christmastime and things like that). The school of composers that followed them, however, was a different proposition altogether. They were called the "*romantics*"—which certainly makes you think. You'd think the capers of Pan and the wandering troubadours and the young Elizabethans with their lutes would take a bit of beating—but no-one had ever thought of giving *them* the title of "romantics".

What They Were Trying To Do

The new school was influenced by two dominant ideas:

(1) Art for art's sake
and (2) Cherchez la femme.

They were dedicated to the task of blending the two ideas, and what with starving in one garret and necking in another they led fairly hectic lives. It is interesting to note (when you read that phrase you can be sure it will be followed by something awfully dull) that many poets and painters and so on were motivated by the same influences (I told you!) at that particular time. There were some shocking goings-on, and you begin to wonder just what got into everybody in the nineteenth century. It isn't as though you can blame it on Hollywood, or the Sunday press, or television.

'Mood Music'

What these composers did (without going into too many details) was to have a bit of a flirtation, then put their feelings into music while they were still in the mood. This music, they discovered, had extraordinary powers; if they then played it over to some other lady, one who wasn't by nature soppy, then she would gradually sort of melt until she jolly well *was*. This was known as *mood* music, but it tended to get rather monotonous, as romantic composers only seemed to have one kind of mood.

'Programme Music'

This kind of thing, though it had its uses, didn't bring in much money, and they started to write *programme* music, that is, the sort that tells a story. Lots of interesting stories they turned out, too, and often they could teach the writers a thing or two in the way of originality. Tchaikovsky, for example, put into music an ingenious little tale called "Romeo and Juliet"—which was all about a boy (Romeo) who had a kind of affair with a girl whose name escapes me for the moment. Then there were the solely descriptive pieces, such as Borodin's "In the Steppes of Central Asia". This illustrates the sound made by a Kurdish caravan procession going past, and experts reckon that it was a brilliant achievement; it seems that the noise made by camels walking in soft sand is one of the most difficult things to do in music. It is also claimed that Rimsky-Korsakov wrote better water-music than Handel, because in "Sadko" you can actually hear the fish. It was Richard Strauss who pretty well put the top hat on programme music; he went and wrote "Don Juan", which was, of course, nothing more nor less than mood stuff—and pretty steamy at that.

Reaction Sets In

There was a violent reaction against the romantics, and a new school sprang up, called the "anti-romantic" school. They reckoned that their predecessors had been kidding all of the people all of the time. They reckoned that there were no such things as chords or harmony—that was just quasi-technical jargon to make the art sound a lot more exclusive than it really was. Further, they argued, you could plonk your hand down on the piano keyboard anywhere you liked and what you got was *music.* "*It is, therefore it is*" was their theory (though possibly I'm getting mixed up with Voltaire, or Einstein) and it made a tremendous impact on the people, who all rushed out and bought pianos with fretted fronts. Some of the anti-romantics are so clever that they write what is called "geometrical music", which is even more difficult than imitating camels walking in soft sand. They love setting problems for one another, such as "prove that the square of the hypotenuse is equal to the sum of the squares of the other two sides, given two cellos and a flute". But the greatest discovery of the anti-romantics is that one straight gin has the same effect on a woman as half-a-dozen dreamy overtures.

Experimental Music

This century quite a lot of musicians have seemed dead set on *proving* things, and it looks as though some of them are going to cut their own throats. They have invented, for instance, a thing called a "colour-organ", which throws colours on to a screen when you play it. When you've seen a certain combination of greys, blues, greens and yellows a good few times, you'll learn to recognize it as "The Bluebells of Scotland". And the time will come when people won't bother *listening* to music at all. Instead of going out in the cold to hear a symphony concert, they'll simply pull a chair up to the fire and fetch out a chart labelled "Haydn's Clock Symphony—Printed by Scawpe and Geach, Docker's Row, London, E.15, under the Supervision of Ted Spratt".

Music Of The Future

A few of the more thoughtful composers are well aware that the orchestra as we know it may eventually disappear, and they are busy making experiments. One of them has just completed a work called "2066 and All That" in which the orchestra consists of only three people, dressed in skins. A woman plays a drum made out of a tree-trunk, the first man performs on a rattle containing pebbles and teeth, and the third man slaps his body.

Music has certainly come a long way since those palaeolithic days. . .

2

Everyday Uses of Music

An Aid To Digestion?

A RUMOUR was started, sometime in the far-distant past, that music helps the digestive processes, but of course you can take that with a pinch of bicarbonate. Anyone who has had to have lunch at the table near the leader of Grzideff's Tzigane Players will know just how dangerous talk of this kind can be.

How Meal-Time Music Started

The idea of having musical accompaniment to meals can be attributed, if you go back far enough, to the rich. Or, to be more precise, the *nouveaux-riches*. In the early days of civilization they had the crazy and rather disgusting notion that money isn't everything. And no matter how rich they were, they never seemed happy; for instance they were incredibly self-conscious about their general lack of manners, but particularly so about the noise they made while eating. The easy way out seemed to have an orchestra play good and loud whenever they had people in for tea. If only they had learned to eat quietly and left it at that, they would have saved a lot of money, kept their friends longer, and spared themselves chronic dyspepsia. Not only that, either; they started something that no-one seems to be able to stop.

As it was, the thing caught on, and soon developed into a cult; anybody who *was* anybody just had to have all these fiddlers and lute-players cluttering up the dining-room.

The First Ship's Orchestra

It got to be an obsession with people, and even those who couldn't stand music had to put up a show, otherwise they were liable to become social outcasts. For instance, when Sir Francis Drake insisted on taking six Corporation musicians with him on his Portuguese expedition, he only had one thing in mind: he wanted to lend an air of respectability to the enterprise. Incidentally, only two of these men came back from that little trip, and Drake never did get round to explaining what had happened to the other four. Probably they thought that Drake had actually wanted them to *play*, and tried serenading him while he was having his corn-flakes on the first morning out. They wouldn't have tried this a second time, not with Drake. None of them could swim, either.

Music In Restaurants

Restaurant music is to be heard in all the best places today, as well as all the worst ones. As a result, sales of indigestion tablets have never been higher, and the drug people are always making jokes about it being an ill-wind. And the restaurateurs aren't grumbling, either, because they know just how useful the orchestra is to them. If the music's bad enough (and it usually is) it helps to take the customers' mind off his food. If the musicians are ugly enough (and they usually are) they can keep him amused during a half-hour wait for his point steak. There will be plenty of food for thought while he's anticipating the other kind . . . (is the old cellist *really* wearing odd socks? And why does the lady pianist blush every time the head waiter passes?).

Covering-Up Music

Another important function of the orchestra is to cover up any undesirable back-stage noises, like the scraping of burnt toast. Worse still are those rows behind kitchen-doors, when a shrill voice accuses one Florrie Baldwin of swiping a welsh rarebit from the hatch, and threatening to report the matter to Mr. Galvani. At times like this, the band can do sterling work with the "Toreador" song, but the snag is that when it stops, the voices of the two ladies are usually twice as loud as when it started.

Musicians As Morale Boosters

One way and another, meal-time music has become a sort of symbol of normalcy, like the Sunday papers, brushing your teeth, and "What's My Line?". Whatever the crisis, from fires to shipwrecks, the band is expected to play on. And when the worst crisis of all comes, and the police swoop on a night club at three a.m., it is the musicians who keep everyone from panicking. Even though they realize that they are out of work from now on, they never fail to reassure the customers with some restful ballad. Like "In Eleven More Months and Ten More Days We'll be Out of the Calaboose".

Who Started Music-While-You-Work?

Many historians reckon that the Greeks were the pioneers of Music While You Work. And it *is* recorded that Bactrian flutes were used during the building of the walls of Messena; but the point is, did they actually *play* them? They may have been used for drainage or something. The writer Ovid later claimed that it was the kindly Romans who first provided music for the workers. When pressed for an illustration, he said, well look at all the cheery jingling and chinking noises the slaves could make with their chains as they tramped towards the mines. Ovid may have been a dab hand at writing passages of "Unseen", but this particular argument seems a bit on the shaky side to me.

Etruscan Experiments

On the face of it, the Etruscans seem to have been far more cultured than either the Greeks or the Romans. *They* had music for practically everything, including boxing-matches. This was very much appreciated by the boxers, who never appeared to get tired. On the other hand, the musicians who accompanied them were all in at the end of each round, and had to be sponged down and fanned with towels. So humane were these Etruscans, that they eventually introduced music for flogging, on the grounds that it would take some of the pain from the punishment. There is little doubt that they were right about this, because when questioned one of the official floggers said: "Oh, definitely. I mean, that pain in my back used to cripple me, now I don't hardly notice it. I can definitely say I enjoy my work much more since they've been using the music of..." (Here he mentioned a well-known firm of Etruscan music publishers.)

Nowadays, of course, the use of music in industry is a highly-specialized art. Among the things the industrial psychologists expect from it is:

The Relief of Boredom. Where once the factory machinist had nothing to do but stare gloomily and silently into a lot of revolving wheels, he can now find all kinds of diversions. "Ah", he might say, "that's a nice bit of French horn playing." "French horn?" says his colleague. "Not a bit of it! A bassoon, that is." The first man is nettled. "Are you trying to tell me I don't know a French horn when I hear it?" And so a lively debate follows, which is only broken up by the arrival of the foreman and the discovery that a lot of bits of metal which oughtn't to have any holes in them are absolutely *riddled* with them. This kind of thing can back-fire, admittedly, but fortunately factory music has another function:

To Minimize Conversation. This is simply achieved. The volume is turned up, so that the music is so loud that the whole joint is jumping (as they say in industrial circles). It is true that everyone gets terrible headaches as a result, not to mention laryngitis from trying to compete with the noise. But if the combination of loud music, headaches, and laryngitis doesn't stop you talking, then you're wasting your time as a machinist. You ought to be an industrial psychologist.

The most important and dramatic use of music, however, is its ability to *CUT DOWN ABSENTEEISM.*

Scene: The bedroom of the Scrivetts' house.

Time: Seven o'clock on a Monday morning in January.

Mrs. S. (*prodding the bedclothes*): Come on, Percy—seven o'clock. I've called you three times already!

Mr. S. (*looks blearily at window. It is snowing outside.*) Huh? Don't think I'll go to work today. Have a sleep in.

Mrs. S. Oh, will you? And what about losing your pay, may I ask?

Mr. S. (*smugly*). Not to worry. I earned enough last week to do us a whole fortnight. Now go away and let me sleep.

Mrs. S. (*is momentarily defeated, then has an inspiration*) All right, Percy. It's a great pity, but you'll have to miss it.

Mr. S. (*from under the bedclothes*). Miss what?

Mrs. S. The Scriabin, of course.

Mr. S. (*his head emerges from bedclothes*). Did you say . . . Scriabin?

Mrs. S. (*casually*). Yes. The factory's putting on his "Prometheus" this morning—had you forgotten?

Mr. S. Wow! (*Throws off bedclothes, springs out of bed.*) Why didn't you say so, woman? You have my breakfast—I can't wait.

(*Dresses frantically. Exit wearing cap, overalls, and carpet slippers, muttering over and over: "Scriabin! Prometheus! Scriabin . . ."*)

Authority's Attitude To Buskers

If you decided to become a street musician today, you probably wouldn't get very far. You'd have the Law on you; you'd be charged with obstructing the traffic, disturbing the peace, and goodness knows what else, and you'd probably have your tin whistle confiscated, too. All this seems a bit rough, especially as it was really the Government who started street music. London corporation used to have its own buskers, and they had to work hard for their money. If the Lord Mayor happened to catch one of them *not* playing, he would be hauled up for obstructing the traffic, disturbing the peace, and so on, and his tin whistle would be confiscated. That's life.

Music For Selling Things Too

One of the difficulties that faced the municipal buskers was finding a place where they could make themselves heard. At one time the towns were absolutely crammed with street traders who felt that they wouldn't be able to sell a thing unless they sang their heads off. Everywhere you went you would hear the strains of "Who Will Buy My Sweet Blooming Lavender?" or "Who Will Buy These Stinking Old Corks?". Sometimes these traders would pinch one another's tunes, and the cleverer ones began inventing very difficult ones so that they couldn't be copied. Unfortunately, they eventually got so difficult that they used to forget the middle bit themselves. It was terribly embarrassing, and all too often they went home at the end of the day without having sold a thing, and with a terrible headache into the bargain. By far the most successful salesman in those times was the man who sold earplugs. And the beauty of it was, *he* didn't have to sing a note.

Dog-music, Pigeon-music, Etc.

Such sounds aren't to be heard any more (no-one seems keen on buying lavender and corks today); and the only officially-recognized music that you are likely to hear in the streets is, strangely enough, *inaudible*. Inaudible, that is, to humans. Someone has invented a very, very high-pitched kind of music, specially designed to chase pigeons away from public buildings, starlings away from cornfields, and dogs away from lady-dogs. It seems to work, too (except perhaps in the latter case; love laughs at tunesmiths, as they say) and the music they use must be marvellously horrible. In fact, if only someone can find a way of translating it into *human* pitch, the inventors will very likely find they've got a whole lot of best-selling Pops on their hands.

Films Depending On Music

Sometimes a film is built around a singer or a musician, and in this case the music doesn't have to be anything special (neither does the acting, or the camera-work, or the direction, or . . .). Someone may decide to make a picture called THE BUDDY SLOUCH STORY. Since Buddy isn't very good-looking, and can't act, an experienced actor usually has to take his part. He has to make himself look fairly ugly, for the sake of verisimilitude (that's a new kind of technicolour) and he must also look as though he can't act—because the *real* Buddy can't act, if you see what I mean. But not to worry, because the *music's* the thing; music's in Buddy Slouch's blood (come to think of it, he *looks* as though he could do with a tonic). For the rest, the film is concerned with the way he rose to the top with no talent whatsoever. It's all very touching until you start asking yourself why you've paid good money to watch someone who hasn't any talent whatsoever.

Function Of Film Music

But music usually has a more *functional* use in films. To start with, it tells you the name of the film company, in case you can't read. That loud, stirring music that comes on right at the beginning tells you right away that you are in for another epic from the EUREKA studios (if you *can* read, you will learn that this musical introduction was composed by someone named Anton Vundernowicz, and this may be true enough. It could be that Mr. Vundernowicz happened to get the idea before Purcell). The next bit of music you hear has another function: to give you the setting of the story:

Setting	*Type of Music*
China, Japan, Siam	Gong, followed by weird chords on xylophone.
South America	Any Latin-American tune played on low notes of marimba.
London	Variations on Big Ben theme, played by horns to suggest fog.

Paris	Perky music with lots of discords, suggesting quick tempers and taxi-cabs. (Alternatively badly-played accordion, suggesting badly-played accordion.)
New York	Tom-toms.

Even though you know who made the film, and where it is supposed to be taking place, you may *still* be hazy as to what it's all about. Eureka Films, however, haven't overlooked that possibility (often enough the Director feels exactly the same way) and to help you there are musical cues, pretty well all the way through:

What's going on	*Type of Music*
Man Falling Downstairs	Xylophone played right to left. Drum.
Murder	Stabbing sort of discord (muted trumpets). Does for *any* type of murder.
Ordinary Death	'Cellos. ("Largo", "After You've Gone". Anything. They all sound the same on a 'cello.)
Came the Dawn	*Sweeping* kind of music (violins and horns). A sort of cross between "Home On The Range" and "Greensleeves".
Sex	Sax.

Many people have been going to the cinema for so long that they can follow a film by the music alone, and they never take much notice of the screen or the dialogue. If it were only the other way about, the film companies would be much happier, especially in these hard times. As it is, they have to pay a hundred musicians for every half-a-dozen actors.

Cutting Down The Expense

Sometimes, however, a director will break with tradition and everything, and cut out all those expensive orchestras. One time, the number of musicians was reduced to *one*, and the picture was a huge success. It was one of those thrilling, *suspense* pictures; it was called "The Third Man" and all the way through you were in a terrible state wondering who this third man was. In the end, it turned out to be the chap who played the zither—a rather pleasant fellow, with glasses.

Music On Television

When television started to become popular, it was thought that music would get quite a boost—but it hasn't turned out that way at all. As a matter of fact you can't get a professional musician to perform in front of those cameras for love or money (well, love, anyway). There are three reasons for this shyness:

1. In many cases he is very versatile, and for years he has been playing in all sorts of different combinations. One day he's Wally Bodger of the New Storeyville Stompers, the next he's playing a mournful 'cello for the Pinkley Spa Orchestra, while on Saturdays he kicks up an awful din with Miguel's Mambo Muchachos at the Lisbon Club. Very, very clever you might think. But he wouldn't look so clever if his Income Tax Inspector were to see him on television seven nights a week.
2. He may be very popular, but he may be a bit shaky on technique. He just dreads the day his more musically-minded fans discover that he's using a style of fingering that went out with the Ark.
3. His face (and he can't help that, bless him).

   (Note: Every now and then you may see an orchestra on your screen whose members look reasonably human and who play quite well, holding their instruments in the correct way and so on. But don't let this fool you. It takes a lot of dubbing and faking to turn out this kind of film, and it's so expensive that it doesn't happen often.)

What Use Is It?

So far the only real use that's been found for music on television has been in the boosting of advertised products. This is rather different from ordinary music, and it must have certain qualifications:

(a) It must be *short* (for example, 2½ seconds is an excellent length, but anything as long as, say, 12 seconds doesn't have much of a chance. Research has proved that the average viewer can't cope with a long, complicated work at one sitting).

(b) The words must be well-nigh unintelligible, with the exception of the last word in each line. And, of course, the name of the product concerned.

(c) It must not sound like *music.*

Cause And Effect

The Jingle-Composers, as they are called (they are also called other names) go to infinite pains to ensure that the jingle is firmly implanted in the mind of the viewer. And often they are far more successful than they realize:

SCENE: The local general-store.

Shopkeeper: Morning, Mrs. Geach—what can I get you?

Housewife: Oh, I'd like a tin of cat food—a tin of er, er, . . . oh, now, *what* do they call it? *You* know—the thing where the Siamese in a top hat plays the banjo . . .

Shopkeeper: (Thinks hard) 'Mm. Top hat . . . banjo. Isn't that SNIF? (Hums)Something, something, half-a-jif,
Something, something, something, SNIF!

Housewife: No, not that one. That's for dogs—SNIF brings out the *man* in your dog! No, this is more lively—sort of Pom-ti-pom-ti-pom-ti-ta,
Pom-ti-pom . . .

2nd Housewife: Excuse me, Mrs. Geach, don't you mean

Pom-ti-pom-ti-oompah—URGE—
Pom-ti-pom-ti-oompah—SPLURDGE!

Shopkeeper: Of course, that's it—Splurdge!

Housewife: Thank you—of course. Yes, it's all come back to me. A tin of Splurdge, please.

Shopkeeper (sadly): Sorry, madam, I don't stock it.

3

Composing and Composers

WHEN WE hear a well-known piece of music—say, Vronsky's trio for two bassoons and a cello—we tend to forget that an awful lot of hard work went into the making of it (as a matter of fact, it's pretty hard work just *listening* to it, but then I don't suppose we *have* to). Just how did the Great Masters set about their most difficult task? (A Great Master, by the way, is pretty well any composer who isn't alive any more.) Well, according to the rules, there are two ways of approaching the business:

How Was It Done?

1. Composing at the piano.

This sounds all right in theory; after all, you've got all the notes in the world right to hand, so to speak. But there are difficulties. For example, you may have invented a passable little minuet, but the *real* problem arises when you start looking around for somewhere to rest the exercise-book in which you are going to write it. If you put it on the music-rest, it wobbles about when you write, and if you lay it on the keys you find that the black ones make the thing terribly bumpy. If these obstacles can be overcome, there's something to be said for composing at the piano, though just at the moment I can't think what.

2. Keeping a sketch-book.

Of course, Beethoven did this, and it's certainly a pleasanter method than the other one. But here again, the composer must make sure it's going to work. There was once an extremely keen and talented young Italian who insisted on carrying his sketch-book around wherever he went for most of his life. Unfortunately it didn't get him anywhere, and he never wrote a single note so far as we know. Mind you, he had a marvellous collection of sketches—people's arms and legs, mostly. Whenever some promising young musician talks of keeping a sketch-book, his tutor is almost bound to quote that Italian as an awful example. Poor old Michelangelo.

Composers' Urge To Get Things Out Of Their Systems

Actually most famous composers weren't very good at sketching (or writing, or doing card-tricks, or anything) and they felt that they had to get things out of their systems through the medium of music. (Incidentally, no-one has ever explained *why* they had to get things out of their systems. The things which they've got out of *their* systems promptly work into those of the simple folk who have paid for the privilege of just listening. It doesn't seem fair, and one of these days someone is going to get up and say so.)

The Franck Technique

What happened in the end, of course, was that most famous musicians threw the book of rules out of the window and went about things their own way. Take César Franck, for example; he used to sit down and play Wagner (straight) for hour after hour. Eventually he would get up, inspired, and start writing feverishly. (Really, I'm only guessing about that "feverishly" but I do know that he used to *write*—I've checked on it.) He got to be very good at this, so much so that I don't imagine that even Wagner could tell the difference if he saw one of those scores—apart from the handwriting, of course. It is rather debatable, however, as to whether it was all worth it; how often do you hear people asking for a copy of "Franck's Lohengrin" or "Franck's Flying Dutchman"? Very seldom.

The Folk-Song Method

Haydn was far more subtle in his approach. He used to listen to the gypsies who came round busking every now and then, and copy down their songs while they weren't looking. Afterwards, when the gypsies were away hop-picking or selling clothes-pegs, he built all those bits of music into larger works. Eventually he finished up with eighty-three string quartets *alone* (I bet that taught him a lesson!). All these were performed many times during his career, and no-one ever doubted that they were all his own work. Gypsies don't go to chamber concerts in the ordinary way, and if they did it might have been a different story. (It might have been a more interesting one, too.)

Schubert's Influences

Whenever anyone asked Schubert who exerted the greatest influence on his work, he always used to say "Shakespeare". People would get quite a shock, because they expected him to say "Haydn" or "Mozart", and they would get out their music encyclopaedias to find out what sort of a musician this chap Shakespeare was. What Schubert used to do was to hand someone a book of Shakespeare's and say: "Open it at any page and give me the first few words". And then, before you could say "Copyright", he would rattle off a brand new song. Two which spring to mind are "Hark, Hark, the Lark", and "Gretchen at the Spinning Wheel". (If you're puzzled by that last one, it's from Shakespeare's play of the same name. I understand it hasn't been published yet, but you should watch out for it. It's one of his best.) Schubert was rather short-sighted and he used to wear his glasses in bed, so they were always breaking. As a result, he didn't see things as other people saw them (that is, when he could see anything at all).

Some critics will have it that there were actually only *two* fish in that stream the day that he wrote the "Trout Quintet", and others swear that they weren't trout at all, but brown carp. It's a pity, really, because a work with a name like "Brown Carp Duet" would sell like hot cakes.

Themes From Everyday Life

It's quite surprising how many composers were inspired by common, everyday things that most of us just take for granted. When we're on holiday for instance, we write home and say "Scenery lovely—weather grand. Just going in for another dip. Back on Saturday". Composers, however, never miss a trick, and when Debussy went for a dip at Ostend, he came up with some little masterpiece like "The Submerged Cathedral". (Note: If you're ever thinking of doing this kind of thing, you'll need a snorkel tube and one of those pens that write under water.)

Mechanical Aid

If you prefer to compose at home, however, you can always use some mechanical aid, like Welcker's Tabular System. According to the label on the box, this enables "any person, without the least knowledge of music, to compose 10,000 minuets in the most pleasing and correct manner". It doesn't say what you're supposed to *do* with 10,000 minuets (I daresay you might run across some publisher who happens to be crazy about minuets. Or just crazy) but at least you'd have the satisfaction of knowing that you'd done them in a pleasing and correct manner.

Once having decided to become a composer, you ought to start *living* like one. All the best composers had one thing in common: they all liked to whoop it up a little.

LISZT

Influence Of Paganini And Women

Liszt was the son of a Hungarian steward, and you can't say that about many people. He didn't get really interested in music (that is, apart from writing a few symphonies and things) until the day he went to Paris to hear Paganini.

When the violinist went into his act, he sat spellbound, which is a very unusual thing for the son of a Hungarian steward to do. "That's it", he thought, "that's the way it should be done—what showmanship!" After the concert, he went round to Paganini's dressing-room to have a word with him, but he couldn't get near the door on account of all those beautiful women. As he watched two of them tearing out one another's hair over a cigarette-end that Paganini had dropped, he was speechless with wonder. Well, *practically* speechless. According to some reports he did go so far as to say "Cor!" and in the circumstances you can hardly blame him.

Liszt's Ambition

This experience left a deep impression on his sensitive mind, and he decided that what Paganini could do with a violin, he could do with a piano. His friends told him he was mad, and he explained that he was only speaking metaphorically. His friends couldn't have been very bright, and I don't suppose they knew what "metaphorically" meant, either. There were a few difficulties at first. There was the problem of how to get over to his audience by using a great heavy thing like a piano. It was all so easy with a violin. You could prance up and down, let your hair flop romantically over your forehead, and pull faces in accordance with the words in italics on the music—dolce, con gusto and the like. You couldn't get these effects by playing the piano facing the audience, because the audience wouldn't be able to see you for the piano, which was always a tall upright at that time.

His Gimmick

What Liszt eventually did (oh, the cunning of the man!) was to insist on having a *grand* piano on the platform. No one seems to have thought of this before. He then practised sitting sort of sideways on, so that everyone could see his finely-chiselled profile and long straight hair. (That was a clever touch, too—most other musicians had long *fuzzy* hair and people were getting sick of it. He used a kind of reverse-

Liszt. Then he practised sitting sideways

action home perm set.) Finally, he learned to introduce his act with a large, gleaming smile and some kind of cosy introduction, like "Why, hallo, everybahdy . . ." This went over big, and very soon Liszt was a household word. Housewives used to go into shops and ask for a giant packet of Liszt. They had no television to educate them in those days.

Women It was just as well that he had all that hair in stock, because everywhere he played, women came clamouring for a lock of it. Their husbands clamoured, too. They clamoured for just one swipe at those finely-chiselled features. Liszt was funny about women. He never went around with girls with names like Betty Ponsonby or Angela Merridew; one day it was George Sand, and the next it was Daniel Stern. These were both females according to him, and *he* should know. Then there was the Polish Princess Carolyne Sayn-Wittgenstein of Weimar who was rather keen on changing her name to his—she had a point there. Another time he got mixed up with a very ordinary young thing named Olga. She was a sweet creature—a Cossack Countess who smoked black cigars and horsewhipped her husband once in a while. Not the kind of girl who stands out in a crowd, you might think, and you'd wonder what Liszt saw in her.

And Children

In spite of all these goings-on, Liszt somehow never got around to marrying anyone, and a lot of his children used to complain about it. They reckoned that their schoolmates were always calling them a rude word. Wagner was Liszt's son-in-law and they often used to wonder how the heck this came about. It couldn't have helped when Wagner found out that he had a mother-in-law named Daniel Stern, and it's no wonder that he gave the whole thing up and wrote all that loud music.

His Secret

Musically, Liszt is famous because he *combined virtuosity with romanticism*. That is, he always played terribly fast so as to get the concert over and sneak off with one of the popsies who were hanging around the stage-door.

MENDELSSOHN

What He Wasn't

Mendelssohn wasn't a charcoal burner's son, and he wasn't born in a humble cottage in the country, and one way and another it's a bit of a mystery how he came to be a composer.

A Backward Child

It's not as though his people were anything special, either. His grandfather was Moses Mendelssohn, the great philosopher, his father was a boringly wealthy banker, and his mother was an artist. Such appalling circumstances would have defeated a lesser man, but Mendelssohn soon determined to overcome his unfortunate background. It was much harder going than he'd imagined, however, and he didn't develop until fairly late in life. He didn't start his first songs until he was turned five, and by the time he was twelve all he'd managed to turn out were a few dozen sonatas and trios and a couple of operas. He used to worry about it, and the day his first big cheque came in he said to his mother: "It's ironic, really, mama. Years ago I could have used this money. I could have spent it on things I treasured—building blocks, foreign stamps, creamy whirls . . . Now at fifteen, these childish things are behind me—what is there left in life?"

"Girls, you dummkopf", said his mother.

The Spirit Of Scotland

He thought this over for a good few years, then got married. His wife stayed home in Germany while he spent his time in England and they were very, very happy. Mendelssohn spent a good deal of time travelling around the country, and probably one of the longest coach-trips he did was the one that took him to Fingal's Cave in the Hebrides. Like all those places that people say you shouldn't miss when you're on holiday, it was rather disappointing—especially as it turned out to be such a wet day. And if he hadn't got so wet, he wouldn't have caught a cold, and then the smart alec who introduced him to the local whisky would no doubt have been disappointed. As it was, he seemed to have got a bit too fond of the stuff, and he is reckoned to be the only composer who's actually written a Scotch symphony. They do say that at one time he embarked on a sort of twin opus dedicated to gin-and-It but he only got as far as the Italian symphony. Goodness knows what amount of liquor he was consuming at this time, but there must have been occasions when he was absolutely speechless during bouts of composing. Look at all those "Songs Without Words".

Royal Patronage

He became quite well-known, however, and he could still play the piano better than most of the characters who played in the pubs. His big moment came when Queen Victoria wrote to him and asked: "When are you coming down to Amuse Us?" That really sobered Mendelssohn, and after

It turned out to be a wet day

that he was always hanging around Buckingham Palace. If Albert thought anything, he never said so. Often in the long winter evenings the Queen would look up from the antimacassar she was knitting and say affectionately (well, *fairly* affectionately): "Come on, Mendy—play something for Us" and the composer, a gentleman to his fingertips, never failed to get up and play something. Mostly it was billiards, and strangely enough Albert always seemed to win.

RIMSKY-KORSAKOV.

Unhappy Back-ground

He was born in the country, in a place called Tikhvin. It was one of those places where everyone from the village blacksmith to the farmer's boy goes around warbling jolly folk-songs the whole time. He daren't say anything, because it might start off a revolution or something, and his father was definitely bourgeois. Eventually, however, all those songs, not to mention the folk, got him down, and he ran away to sea and grew a great long beard.

The Composer At Sea

Imagine his horror when he found he had jumped from the frying pan into the fire. All day long he had to put up with the wailing of concertinas and very semi-skilled renderings of "Blow The Man Down" and "Vodka For My Ivan-O". It was awful, and he took to locking himself in his cabin. In desperation, he tried doing a spot of composing of his own in order to take his mind off the terrible din that was going on outside. Actually, he got the idea from a rather tatty book called "Spare Time Composing For Fun And Profit" which he'd picked up in the ship's library. He didn't do too badly, either, considering that there were quite a few pages missing.

An Inspired Symphony

One time his ship was laid up for three months at Gravesend (his captain was having a long week-end) and Rimsky-Korsakov decided to pass the time away by writing a symphony. It was a *descriptive* symphony, inspired by all the queer fish he'd encountered during those three months. This is rather interesting, because if he'd stayed aboard instead of going to parties given by queer fish, that wonderful work might never have been written. Doesn't that thought just stagger you? (If it doesn't, don't worry too much about it. Sometimes people ask if you think History would have taken a different turn if Cleopatra's nose had been half-an-inch longer. Of course it would—plastic surgery would have been invented a couple of thousand years sooner. This kind of hypothesis gets you nowhere; you might as well wonder what might have happened if Rimsky-Korsakov wrote "Chopsticks". Half-a-minute, though—he *did* write "Chopsticks". Come to think of it, so did Liszt and Borodin and Cui and Lyadov. So help me, they *all* wrote "Chopsticks"—only they called it "Paraphrases" so as not to offend the Chinese authorities, who were trying to get people to use knives and forks at that time.)

Rimsky-Korsakov's Genius For Titles

Why, you may ask, did the composer call this particular symphony "Sadko"? Well, you can just imagine him, after he'd completed the final bars, looking round for a title. Of course, there was really only one place he could look, and that was through the porthole. And there, opposite, he sees a great warehouse wall bearing the words "SOUTHAMPTON AND AVONMOUTH DREDGING CO." It's not such a bad title, though it *is* a bit on the long side, and so Rimsky-Korsakov telescoped it into "SADKO". It wasn't his fault that he always spelt "Co." with a K. The fellow was Russian, dammit.

A Foolish Mistake

He wrote every kind of music, from chamber-music to opera, and two of his most successful works were "The Maid of Pskov" and "Ivan the Terrible". But a strange thing happened the first time "Ivan the Terrible" was performed. A lot of people got up and said to themselves: "Good heavens, I saw this at the Berlin Opera House" and went home rather puzzled. You couldn't blame them, because it *was* supposed to be a first performance. There were a lot of complaints, and Rimsky-Korsakov suddenly realized he'd gone and written the same opera twice, with different titles. He was extremely apologetic but he refused to give anyone their money back. He reckoned he'd put all those hours in just the same, and mumbled something about the "rate for the job". (This was years before the revolution, too.)

The Big "Five"

Eventually he was discharged from the Navy without a stain on his character. This was a pretty serious business in those days, but the Admiralty said they'd let it go this time. Just to be on the safe side, though, he joined the famous "Five", together with Balakirev, Borodin, Mussorgsky, and our old friend Cui. These men were sort of musical detectives, bent on cleaning up the country. They were quite successful, too; between them they cleaned up a few million roubles in next to no time.

Importance Of Colour To Rimsky-Korsakov

Rimsky-Korsakov was especially well-known for his "colourful" music. As a matter of fact, he didn't recognize colours as such—he only saw them as musical chords. When he was buying a new tie, he's say: "That's too B flat—have you got something with a bit more A major in it?" He wasn't being uppish—he just couldn't help it. But a lot of pseudo-intellectuals took the thing up as a sort of cult, and pretty soon it got that way that you couldn't get a job as tie-salesman in St. Petersburg unless you had your cap and gown. Other composers used to laugh at this idiosyncrasy of Rimsky-Korsakov's, but it was largely a question of sour grapes. Actually, most of them were E minor with envy.

HAYDN

Musical Beginnings

Haydn was different from a lot of composers because he was of *gentle birth* (that is, the midwife never dropped him on his head or anything). Unlike Rimsky-Korsakov, he really *liked* the local folk-songs. He was born in a wheelwright's cottage, and he was very fond of listening to the music of the gypsies who used to defy the "NO HAWKERS OR MUSICIANS" notice on the garden gate. He soon learned lots of songs, and at a very early age he used to accompany himself quite competently on the cart-wheel. His father was always ticking him off for this, though in later years he didn't feel so badly about it. He admitted that though he used to find a lot of his new wheels badly buckled, they were always beautifully in tune.

Haydn Not Very Good At Maths.

Although he was so clever musically, Haydn wasn't very good at maths. What with not being able to count very well and writing so many hundreds of works, Haydn used to keep forgetting what opus he was up to. So he started giving his symphonies nicknames, like the "Clock" or "Mit Dem Hornersignal" or "Nellie Dean". Even then he used to get mixed up, and eventually he gave the whole thing up and wrote "Il Distratto" (The Absent-minded Person).

His Sense Of Humour

He was very fond of playing little jokes on his musicians, like writing passages for the trumpet that couldn't be played on a trumpet; and having the French horn players breathing in and out at the same time. Trumpeters and French horn players thought he was a scream, and they used to call him affectionate names like "bonehead" and "sonofabitch". He was also called "The father of the symphony" but never took offence at that either. Only when someone referred to him as "the Robert Burns of Croatia" did he take umbrage; he pointed out that the only curves that had influenced *his* work had been on the rims of cart-wheels.

4

Instruments

Reasons For Changes

THE NUMBER and range of instruments have increased from time to time through the ages, because musicians will keep on inventing ways of making noises that were once thought to be quite impossible. As a matter of fact, some critics *still* think they are quite impossible. At the same time, however, various other instruments have been thrown over for one reason or another. It may have been because no-one could get any sort of tune out of them; or because they tended to fall to pieces when you started playing them (which can be rather disappointing, especially if you haven't finished the instalments). On the face of it, they don't seem such bad reasons at that.

Nature's Fight Against Increase Among Instruments

It's an ill wind, however, and if it hadn't been for this gradual discarding of unsatisfactory instruments, there would be a ridiculous number of them around today. Composers would go crazy (all right, then—*crazier*) trying to work them all into their orchestrations, and an average symphony orchestra would run to about fifteen hundred players. Whichever way you look at it, this is far too many players. Half of them would have to stand in the aisles, and the conductors (you couldn't have less than four) wouldn't so much be keeping time as *order*. You can imagine how dreadfully self-conscious the audience would feel, being so outnumbered and sort of hemmed in, and what with one thing and another, the whole thing would get completely out of hand. It's just as well that Kindly Old Nature has stepped in to preserve the balance, improving on Art like anything. To beat the band, in fact.

Do We Need More Than One Instrument?

It is universally accepted (actually, I haven't checked with the Martians yet; I'm expecting to hear any day now) that it is a good thing that everyone doesn't play the same instrument, but there are a few dissenters, not to mention those who don't agree. For example, I've often thought that "The Eton Boating Song" could be made jolly interesting if performed by a band of about two dozen euphoniums. There would be snags, of course, as in every branch of experimental art. There'd be trade union trouble for a start; and I can just hear them asking "Who OOMPS in the OOM-PAH?" This is a difficult question to answer, and thinking it over I think I'll shelve this idea till the time seems ripe.

Types Of Instrument

How many types of instrument are there? You are probably familiar with the three main groups (if not, then you'd better *get* familiar pretty quick, because I'm going to go into some rather technical stuff very shortly).

Group No. 1. Strings (plucked or scraped).
" " 2. Brass and Woodwind (blown or sucked).
" " 3. Percussion (banged or bonged).

Idiophones

N.B. You may think that these groups would cover just about everything. But not so. There *is* another group (don't let it get around) called the *idiophone* group. It includes all those things which are *not* plucked, scraped, blown, sucked, banged or bonged. Idiophones are, in fact, struck, shaken, stamped on, scratched, and kicked around generally. They sound rather jolly, and it might be an idea to get a few friends together and form your own little orchestra. You won't get much in the way of music, but by the time the next Olympic Games come round you'll have a tough little team that ought to be able to beat anyone at anything.

Danger Of Crossing Violin Bridges Before They Are Reached

Many parents make the mistake of choosing an instrument for their children while they are still at school. This is a terrible chance to take. The child in question may detest the violin, or whatever it may be. What's more, after the first few lessons, the parents will detest it, too. Very soon, they will detest the child, who will in turn detest them; while the tutor will detest all three. All this detesting and everything can be very distressing, yet it can so easily be avoided. If only the parents in such cases tried learning the violin themselves before inflicting it on someone else, they would soon find out how impossible the whole thing was, and start on a model railway or something instead.

Caution In Choosing Instrument

Even supposing that a young person is genuinely keen to tackle a certain instrument (some people have the *strangest* children) then he or she would still be well-advised to wait a few years before making a decision. The reason is, that no-one knows exactly what size or shape he's going to finish up. Anyone who seems to be sticking at four foot seven, for example, should give the double bass a wide berth (Note: ships' musicians should do this regardless of their height). It's bad enough having to cart one of these things around everywhere, without having to carry along a step-ladder as well.

Pitfalls For Fat People

Very fat people should be particularly careful in their choice of instrument. Some of them spend their life's savings on an ebony piano, only to find it's a white elephant. This is brought home to them every time they sit down at it, and everyone laughs because they are not really *at* it except in the very widest sense of the term. Again, it should be a simple matter to try the instrument in the shop before buying it, when it ought to be obvious whether or not their hands are going to reach the keyboard. Or whether they can even *see* the keyboard, come to that. Here is an easy-to-remember rule for fat, musically-minded people: IF the diameter of the waist exceeds the distance between the armpit and the finger-tips, then play safe and take up the piccolo.

Other Physiological Factors

In the same way, a man who lashes out four or even five pounds on a brand-new Stradivarius despite the fact that he has no chin to tuck it under is just throwing his money away. If he was *really* keen—practically fanatical, in fact—he might go in for a spot of plastic surgery, though on second thoughts it might be less inconvenient to have the violin remoulded. But then it wouldn't be a violin, and where do we go from there? There's only one answer to this kind of situation: the man in question ought to risk the additional expense and buy a mouth-organ instead. He should find endless scope here. With no chin to get in the way, he should be able to develop some brilliant wrist-work and achieve a speed which people with chins can only dream about. As Confucius says: Better to be a virtuoso on the mouth-organ than just so-so on the fiddle.

What And Where?

You'd think that people who go and buy a biggish sort of instrument would first consider

1. Where they are going to keep it,

and 2. How they are going to get it there.

But then musical types are not renowned for their practicality (off-hand, I can't think of anything they *are* renowned for. Most of them aren't even renowned for their music. However . . .) and it's estimated that the number of grand pianos more or less permanently jammed half-way up lighthouses is quite extraordinary.

That popular organist, Reggie Schmaltz, never tires of telling the story (actually, he's sick to death of it—it's the publicity he never tires of) of how he got involved with this second-hand Wurlitzer (the advertisement had said: "Suit

Importance Of Finding Suitable Home For Instruments

learner"). It seems it wasn't until the thing had arrived in the street that he began to have his doubts. You see, he lived in a tenth-storey attic. A *back* attic. He was quick to see the difficulty, however, and after a while he stopped trying to take it to bits and had the men deliver it to his uncle's farm, way out in the country. And that week-end, he went to live there. That is, he went to live in the Wurlitzer. He often recalls how happy he was there, the only snag being the crows that used to keep building nests in the pipes. The only thing that would keep them away was "In A Persian Market" played fortissimo, before and after meals. He reckons it was all this practice that got him where he is today.

"In A Persian Market" may be the only thing he can play—but he can play it louder than anyone else in the world.

Identification

Let us suppose that you have taken expert advice, grown your hair long, and said goodbye to your friends; you have, in short, decided on a certain instrument. The question now is, do you really know anything about it? To start with, will you be able to recognize it when you see it? This is terribly important, because you may get into an awful lot of trouble if you pick up the wrong instrument by mistake. A lot of people, for instance, confuse the trumpet with the trombone, which is quite understandable because they both make a noise like a sick cow when you blow them for the first time. You may come away with a trombone, thinking it was a trumpet; and before long you will imagine that the thing is coming to pieces, and you will either send it back to the makers with a nasty letter or spend a small fortune on a lot of unnecessary repairs.

This sort of thing shouldn't happen to a dog (not even a circus dog) and it is hoped that the following facts about a few popular instruments, carefully picked at random, will prove helpful. (Note: It may be that having read these notes, you will go right off the instrument you had in mind, and perhaps all the others as well. This may depress you for a while, but at least there's a chance you may regain the friendships you recently abandoned. It's an ill wind.)

THE BAGPIPES

There seems to be some doubt as to where the bagpipes originated, and what's more you get very little help when trying to get a few facts. We know that they were used by all kinds of people—the Hittites and the Romans and the Greeks and the Bretons and the Norwegians and the Persians and the Irish and the Welsh. One or two have even been heard as far afield as Scotland. But the point is, who had them first? The Romans blamed the Hittites, the Irish say it was the Welsh, and so on. The truth is, no-one will own up to it, although it was recently claimed in "Pravda" that the Russians were the first *not* to have bagpipes. I think that's all that can be said on the subject of origins. The name itself has suffered a lot of changes through the centuries. (William Shekspyre had the same trouble, if you remember.) The poorer type of street musician referred to their BEG-PIPES; while the BIG-PIPE was a formidable, dual-purpose instrument much favoured by the Scots. They used to hit the English over the head with it. When the superstitious Irish were troubled by the Evil Ones as they haunted the marshes at night, they would set out to chase them away with their BOG-PIPES. Just as essential so far as the nineteenth-century Londoners were concerned were the BUG-PIPES; *they* used to have visitors in the night, too. There might have been a lot more variants of the bagpipe, and perhaps it's just as well that there are only five vowels in the language.

THE CWRTH

This hasn't the same scope as the bagpipes; in fact when it comes to vowels, it doesn't even get a look-in. But it does at least have *one* distinction, because it is reputed to be the oldest instrument to be played with a bow.

The name itself is probably an attempt (and a jolly good one, as I think you'll admit) to reproduce the noise made when a bow is drawn slowly across the strings *from left to right*, thus: CWRTH . . . (I should have said that another distinction is its peculiar ability to Set People's Teeth On Edge.) And here's an interesting thing: if you pull the bow *back* again—i.e., from right to left—the sound that comes out goes something like HTWRC . . . And this, believe it or not, is CRWTH spelt backwards. It's certainly a funny world. The last time anyone played a CWRTH in public, either from left to right or vice-versa, was in 1801. From the looks of things it seems to be losing its popularity.

THE PIANO

For a long time the only suitable instrument for accompanying purposes was the harp, but most men hated having to play it because they thought it was rather effeminate. Besides, it had a serious snag: if you happened to put your foot down on one of the pedals by mistake, then the pitch of the thing was suddenly raised by two semitones! This kind of thing can be terribly embarrassing. Then came the harpsichord, which was more efficient in the matter of pedals (sometimes they even had starting-handles for emergencies, too) and looked a little more masculine. In fact, some ladies resented this, and a special *feminine* kind of harpsichord was invented. These were called virginals, which is just about as feminine as you can get. But there was a snag here, too. The strings had to be plucked with quills, and they kept getting clogged up with feathers. Obviously something tougher was called for, but there again everything they tried seemed to be feminine—needles, thimbles and so on.

At last some clever male (actually, he was a hammer-maker from Eastcheap) suggested that the strings ought to be *hit*, not plucked, and that's how the piano came on the scene. There have been pianos of all shapes and sizes, specially designed for ships, cottages, and what have you.

Nowadays, there are, generally speaking, only two main types—the UPRIGHT and the GRAND. Beginners often ask, what is the difference? Well, one is as good as another, really—it's rather like trying to compare a coupé with a saloon car. However, you may be interested to know that in an upright model, the strings run *vertically*, while in the grand they are always *horizontal*. This is just as well, because if it was the other way round, both instruments would have a ghastly shape. Since the grand is very much an off-the-floor model it has certain advantages: apart from being able to push drunks underneath it at parties, you will find it presents little difficulty when you're cleaning the carpet. In fact, some say that this is the main reason for its popularity; they reckon that the first grand to be used in a private household was bought by an Alsatian baron for his wife because she was so house-proud. When she saw it, she was delighted, and exclaimed "Ee, lad, it's grand!" (it seems she came from Rochdale) and somehow the name stuck.

The best thing you can do so far as the upright type is concerned, however, is to have the carpet fitted around it. Nothing will move it, once it is installed, except dry rot in the floorboards. On the other hand, it is ideal for displaying framed photographs and those little china dogs whose tails droop when it's raining. Before the days of electricity, these pianos used to have candlesticks fitted to the front. But they were more trouble than they were worth so far as the pianist was concerned: smoke used to get in *his* eyes years and years before Jerome Kern thought of the idea. Admittedly, every model had its dampers, but apparently that didn't help much, and what with one thing and another most people gave the instrument a wide berth. The composers of the nineteenth century wrote hundreds and hundreds of symphonies, and often scored for such unusual instruments as hand-looms and gun-cannons. But do any of these symphonies contain one single note for the piano? (Well, *you* can answer that one by wading through all the nineteenth-century symphonies. You can report back in about fifteen years.)

Even so, the piano was for a long time a sort of focal point for the family. They were always gathered round it—on weekdays to look at their photographs, and to see whether the china dog's tail was sticking up or down. On Sundays they would sing hymns and pray. The younger ones used to pray for all sorts of things, such as dry rot in the floorboards and the coming of television. These prayers came true, especially the second one. And nowadays, when you ask someone if they want to buy a piano (or rather, if they would like it as a gift, carriage paid), they are liable to ask: "How many channels?"

THE PSALTERY

You don't sound the P, and, of course the name speaks for itself. The box in which grocers used to keep their salt was a shallow, oblong affair, and eventually a man named Pjones got the idea of stretching wires across the top and using it as a cheese-cutter as well. It worked well enough, except that bits of cheese would keep falling down into the salt. But this was a blessing in disguise because a lot of his customers thought it was real Stilton on account of that nice tangy flavour. It was probably while he was fishing out these bits of cheese that Pjones discovered the musical properties of his gadget.

You play the psaltery by plucking the wires with some kind of plectrum (that is, a thing you pluck wires with). If you haven't a plectrum, you could use the end of a cheese-knife. Come to that, you needn't pluck the thing at all if you don't feel like it. That's the beauty of the psaltery—you can always use it to keep salt in.

SCACCIAPENSIERI

The proper name for this instrument, of course, is the JEW'S HARP, but some people find JEW'S HARP difficult to pronounce. It is a sort of small steel frame, with a springy bit of steel in the centre. You play it by resting it against the teeth, opening the mouth slightly (not *too* wide, unless you want to swallow the thing) and then twanging the springy bit of steel. Oh, and it's as well to sort of roll your tongue into a ball before you start, otherwise you'll be talking with a lisp for ages. Very soon you'll have managed to arrive at the Note (a Jew's Harp only has one note, but it's quite a nice one. Better one nice note than a hundred nasty ones, I always say) and perhaps one day you'll become a virtuoso like Eulenstein. Eulenstein, by the way, was never happy with less than sixteen Jew's Harps all twanging away, and if no-one christened him "Satchel-Mouth" then his manager wasn't trying.

The Jew's Harp seems to have originated in places like Japan and Borneo and New Guinea, and was most widely used by the Thick-Lipped races. (Originally they were mostly Thin- or Medium-Lipped, but that was before they took to the Jew's Harp.) It is cheap and easy to maintain, and the only expenditure you are likely to incur is the cost of renewing a few teeth every so often. (N.B. The instrument is also known as the Maultrommel, the Styrmant, and the Trompe de Laquais. People find it *terribly* hard to say JEW'S HARP.)

THE VIOLIN

This instrument was adapted from the older VIOL by the

Amati family of Cremona, in Italy. I don't want this to get around, but in the process of adaptation they made a bit of a mess of things. First of all, they forgot to put two of the strings on it (so that it only had four instead of six), and then, even worse, they didn't put any metal frets on the fingerboard to denote where the various notes were! However, the violinists of that time were a proud lot, and they pretended that it didn't make any difference to *them*. Actually, the new instrument was a boon to them, especially those that weren't very good, because if you didn't happen to hit the right place first time, you could sort of slide your finger along the wood until you found it. With the viol, this kind of thing only resulted in a miserable PLINK! and gave you awful blisters into the bargain. It just wasn't worth it.

The two squiggly holes in the body of the instrument have not been put there for fun, as anyone who has ever tried to make squiggly holes in things will well know. They are there, in fact, to enable you to see the Stradivarius label stuck inside (*all* violins, incidentally, should have a Stradivarius label stuck inside: if yours hasn't, you should take it back to the dealers and get your three pounds fifteen refunded). How the labels get there seems to be something of a trade secret, like ships in bottles.

Another mystery is why there are still *four* strings on the violin. You'd have thought that they'd have decreased in number in this streamlined age, and anyone who has heard a one-stringed fiddle will agree that one is enough. More than enough. It could be that the three on the left are sort of reserves, in case the E breaks. You will notice that they get stouter as you go from right to left, and the third reserve—the outside-left—is a real fatty. This is the G string, and it will stand *anything*, even being worn by a strip-artist.

Sometimes a thing called a MUTE is clipped over the bridge of the violin, with the idea of making it noiseless.

But, ingenious though this gadget is, it is far from being a hundred per cent efficient. You could clip on *six* mutes, and, so help me, you'd *still* be able to hear the violin.

It is claimed that there are *over seventy* parts to a violin, and you may find this hard to believe. But if you've ever sat on one at a party, you'll know that this is an understatement, if ever there was one.

5

Conducting

BEFORE THE present method of conducting was arrived at, many other ways had been tried out. Among these were

(1) Stamping on the floor,

(2) Conducting with a roll of music from an organ-seat, and (3) Waving a violin-bow.

The Foot Technique

You can imagine that stamping on the floor would be quite satisfactory, especially if the platform were a nice, hollow-sounding one. You could start up a fine old *boom, boom, boom,* and everyone could join in and have a jolly good time. Everyone, perhaps, except the orchestra. They probably couldn't make themselves heard, and this must have made a lot of them tend to lose interest in their work.

It Didn't Last

Foot-conducting was eventually abandoned, and you might be interested in the story of how it came about (whether you are or not, it's coming up just the same). It seems that an up-and-coming French conductor, whom we shall call Le Grimbaud, was once conducting a concert in honour of Louis XIV's birthday. The king was, as usual, sitting in the middle of the front row. Unthinkingly, he put his hat on the edge of the platform . . . (strangely enough, they had no cloakrooms then—now we have cloakrooms but no cloaks). Anyway, as Le Grimbaud started stamping his right foot, the vibration caused the hat to edge its way quietly across the stage. The next thing that Louis knew, there it was, right underneath the conductor's raised foot. He upped and shouted "Ma Chapeau!" (Imagine! Every schoolboy knows that "chapeau" is masculine. It just shows how frantic the king must have been.) But it was too late. By the time Le Grimbaud had said "Quoi?" his foot had crashed down. That was the end of (a) the hat, (b) Le Grimbaud, and (c) foot-conducting.

Beethoven's Substitute System

Some conductors, like Beethoven, were hard task-masters, and the weaker members of the orchestra had to drop out during rehearsals. And when it came to the public performance, even the hardier ones would begin to flag. They would go suddenly glassy-eyed and start dropping like guardsmen on a summer parade. Not unnaturally, this caused a fair amount of inconvenience; there would be sudden bouts of silence in the middle of a symphony, and people started putting their coats on, thinking the concert was over. Even Beethoven, who was a bit short-sighted and hard of hearing, began to notice things, and he decided to have no more of it. He had his organ brought forward a bit, and began conducting from the seat—the idea being that, as soon as a player dropped out, he would pull out the appropriate stop (flute, bombardon, etc.) and take over that man's part. He got so good at this that the audience seldom knew the difference. Unfortunately, this practice brought out the worst in some of the musicians, and they sometimes took advantage of the master's virtuosity (not to mention his myopia) by breaking off here and there for a smoke or a quick game of pontoon.

Still, it all made a change, and Beethoven was very much in demand as a conductor. He was always improving his

Snags Of Conducting From Organ

organs, and the tale is told of a very special one he once had built for a very important concert in Heidelberg. Apparently, he was pretty busy with rehearsals and never got round to inspecting the job before it was completed. And when he got to the hall on the night of the concert he found that the organ builders had sort of overdone things. He had to use a twenty-foot ladder to get up to the seat; and when he got there he found it was an awful long way from the orchestra. It wasn't just that he couldn't hear them (he could get round that)—he couldn't even *see* them. He cupped his hands around his mouth and tried to explain his dilemma, but of course no-one could make out what he was saying. In fact, the leader took it to be a signal to start, and they all plunged into the overture. Beethoven couldn't make out what was going on, and was just about to come down again when someone took the ladder away. No-one is sure just how he passed the time for the two hours he was stranded there. According to some reports he used his roll of music as a pea-shooter and got his own back on some of the musicians, but as one eminent critic has pointed out, where would he get the peas? Anyway, he couldn't have been in a very good temper when they let him come down at the interval. And he must have felt worse when he read in the papers next morning that all the critics thought the concert tailed off in the second part, though before the interval the orchestra had played together with "an uncanny, almost military, precision".

Violin-Bow Method

When some of the other conductors learned what happened that night in Heidelberg, they decided that from then on, organs were definitely out for conducting from. As it was still necessary for them to boost up the score themselves, they thought they'd try conducting with the bow of a violin, keeping the instrument in the other hand in case of emergency. This brought them much closer to their men, and their men weren't a bit happy about it. There were no more Pat and

"Had a tendency to lash out with the violin bow"

Mike stories during concerts, no more sly games of pontoon. Worse, the more temperamental conductors had a tendency to lash out with the bow at any player who happened to make a mistake. Now the violin bow is so constructed, that once you get your ear entangled between wood and horse-hair it's very difficult to extract it. Many an unfortunate musician has learned just *how* difficult, and many a conductor found that an awful lot of time was wasted in disentangling things. You'd have thought they would have stopped lashing out at people and left it at that. But no—they didn't want to be taken for softies. Instead they started using a straight up-and-down piece of wood which they could still hit people with (or throw at them) but which was easier to handle. They

Invention Of The Baton

began paying more attention to these things than they gave to the music. And nowadays conductors have lost the art of playing organs, violins and everything else; it takes them all their time to pick out "Chopsticks" at parties.

Why 'Baton'?

They are, however, experts with the baton, and they are all pretty smug about it. Incidentally when someone once asked Toscanini why it was called a baton, he got annoyed and said, "Well, it *looks* like a baton, don't it?" In music, the answers to questions that seem imponderable are often so very simple.

HOW TO BECOME A CONDUCTOR

Q. What is the first thing I must do to become a conductor?

A. Well, first of all, you'll have to think about a name. You can't just have any old name if you want to join the ranks of immortal genius. Supposing, for instance, that your name is O'Brien—that will never do. You must change it right away. From now on you are Obrienovitch, the brilliant son of a poor Latvian cobbler. After a humble childhood in the village of . . .

Q. Just a minute—suppose my name *is* Obrienovitch already—what then?

A. Eh?

Q. I said, suppose my name *is* . . .

A. I'm glad you brought that up. Come to think of it, it *is* a pretty common name. The music profession is probably lousy with Obrienovitches already. Tell you what—change it to O'Brien.

Q. But you said . . .

A. Never mind what I said. There's nothing wrong with O'Brien, nothing at all. Perfect, no nonsense about it. Suggests simplicity, aggressiveness and Celtic fire.

Q. Is it essential, then to have Celtic fire?

A. Oh, no—at least, it needn't be Celtic. You can have French fire, Italian fire, Spanish fire and so on. But *not* English fire—that's definitely out.

Q. Are you saying that Englishmen are more or less barred from the rostrum?

A. Bless you, no. It's just that it's more difficult for them to become celebrities. They have to be so terribly English, you wouldn't believe. They can be clean-shaven and dapper or droopy and whiskery; they must be impatient, bad-tempered, witty, kindly, eccentric and very good at T.V. panel games.

Q. It's more complicated than I thought. But assuming that I have all the qualifications, how could I learn the actual technicalities of the job?

A. You simply find yourself a tutor—there are plenty of them in the big towns. You may have seen their adverts. in little boxes on the back pages of boys' magazines. You know the kind of thing . . . "THEY LAUGHED WHEN HE PICKED UP HIS BATON!"

Q. Have you any idea what form the lessons will take?

A. You will be taught, for a start, the separate functions of the hands. For instance, the right hand, you'll find, controls the beat and the tempo; while the left looks after things like dynamics and agogics.

Q. What's an agogic?

A. That's a very good question, and I'm glad you asked it. Now you are probably also wondering what happens when you want to leave the tempo alone for a bit, while you want to put the orchestra right over its dynamics. Or it might be vice-versa. This is where your tutor will make you practise with one hand tied behind your back.

Q. Why is that?

A. So that you will learn how to conduct with one hand without falling over.

Q. Is there any danger of this?

A. Every danger. But don't worry—the audience love it. Get them on your side and it's half the battle. Now what about some more technicalities. Oh, yes. Did you know that the concert platform should have a "rake", or tilt, away from the auditorium?

Q. No. And I suppose there is a reason for that, too?

A. There is. If your baton should happen to fly out of your hand during a bit of accelerando, then it will always roll back to you. By the way, you should make sure the "rake" isn't too steep, otherwise you'll have the big drum rolling over you in the middle of Ravel's "Bolero". You wouldn't like to be *drummed* out of the profession would you, ha, ha?

Q. Ha, ha. Is that everything, then?

A. Heavens, no. You'll have to make sure everyone turns up at rehearsals—and, incidentally, I hope your arithmetic's good. It's not easy counting people who are hiding behind instruments, especially organs. And there's always the odd, incorrigible cellist who skips from chair to chair to cover up for his pals who are still in the boozer.

Q. It seems one must be something of a disciplinarian.

A. Yes, but don't take it too far. You'll also be a sort of welfare officer, too. You will learn to listen with sympathy to the problems of your men, especially those concerning the urgent need of a fiver till pay-day. Occasionally you'll have to grant compassionate leave to a double-bass player whose wife has run off with a piccolo-player. This is always happening to double-bass men, and it's just another ugly sidelight on the housing problem.

Q. Well, thank you—I'm sure I've learned a lot. Just one more thing, though. What *is* an agogic?

A. Agogics, if you must know, represent graduations which affect intensity, such as the calculated use of the rallentando and tempo rubato and accelerando and fermatas. In other words, without agogics you're a dead duck. Does that make it plain?

Q. Ah, well, ask a silly question and you get a silly answer.

6

Military Bands, Brass Bands and Silver Bands

Is There a Difference?

PEOPLE OFTEN ask, what is the difference between a military band, a brass band, and a silver band? In each case, they argue, the members wear uniforms and blow down things—and, of course, this is quite true up to a point. But there *are* differences, and if we take a look at the history of blown music these will become obvious.

Development Of Military Music

We've seen that music has always been used for war, though for a long time no-one regarded the stuff they used to play as *music proper;* in fact it was very often the reverse. Pieces like "Come to the Cookhouse Door, Boys" and "Reveille" were all very nice, but the critics felt that there wasn't an awful lot you could say about them. Then, as time went on, soldiers began introducing all kinds of fancy instruments, like whiffles and trommelflöte and serpents. They made the drums bigger, and they brought out the "hautbois", which means "high wood". (When it was first introduced, the C.O. of a famous London regiment showed it to his men and said: "Who would like to try this new instrument?"

Their attempts
were a bit amateurish

And, we are told, a little cockney stepped smartly forward and said "Hi would, sir".)

Some soldiers got very musically-minded, and used to put jolly words to the bits they played, such as—oh, well, never mind. And when they were eventually demobbed, and their nice shiny trumpets taken from them, they were liable to go into tantrums. Their sergeants had an awful job soothing them.

Trombones Into Ploughshares

But these chaps just *had* to express themselves, and the time came when some of them hit on the idea of carrying on their music in Civvy Street. The trouble was, they had to make their own instruments, and to start with their work was a bit on the amateurish side. They had difficulty in remembering how many times round you have to wind a French horn, or whether the bell of the euphonium points *towards* or away *from* the player. A lot of other things went wrong, too. When, for instance, they played the note *C* on the soprano cornet, what came out every time was *E Flat*. And when they tried this same note on the euphonium, what do you think they got? You'll never guess—*B Flat*, so help me. No-one could fathom this out; it looked as though someone's tuning-fork had been used for opening tins of bully beef or something. Anyway, the first time they all got together for a session, the noise was pretty awful, and round about that time the Army started getting letters from hysterical women, asking that their husbands be taken back to barracks forthwith.

Brass Hats v. Brass Bands

Now the army authorities were enraged when they found out what these ex-servicemen were doing. As far as they were concerned, this kind of blown-music was sacrosanct. Right away, they tried to push a bill through parliament, forbidding it to be played by civilians. The ex-servicemen retaliated just as quickly. They stopped going to Annual camp and the Friday Olê-Tyme dances at the T.A. barracks. Soon the thing became a political issue, with questions being asked in the House about "this aesthetic cruelty to our boys", and what with one thing and another, the War Office just had to back down. However, they did manage to place certain restrictions on brass-bands, as they later came to be called.

According to the new regulations, civilian instruments were to be coated with brass to distinguish them from military ones. What's more, they could only be played in

(1) A place where the public could neither see them nor hear them. E.g., a coal mine.

(2) A building where there was so much row going on already that no-one would be able to tell what they were playing (or even if they *were* playing). E.g., a motor works.

(3) The middle of a large open space—on condition that some kind of fence or rail were erected to keep people from getting too near. E.g., a public park.

These regulations are, of course, still more or less obeyed. And that's why, if you wanted to hear a brass-band tonight (well, you *might*) you'd have to go to a colliery or a motor works. In the nice weather, of course, they're allowed to play in the park; but the rails are still there, and it isn't advisable to feed the musicians. They get tea and buns from the Council; and there's talk of a pretty liberal boot-allowance which ought to stop sympathizers from throwing pennies into the stand.

Gulf Between Brass And Military Bands

There is still a lot of resentment among the musicians, for all that. There they are, they complain, stuck down coal-mines and so on, while their counterparts, the military men, can play *just wherever they please*. They can hold up the traffic in the streets, they can hold up the game at football matches, and—this is what gets the brass boys blazing mad—they can tootle out the Veleta at the T.A. dances and get paid for it. It's anyone's guess how long this unequal situation will continue, but every now and then the brass-bandsmen from all over the country have mass-meetings under the cunning guise of band contests! And the day isn't far off when there's going to be a show-down.

The Difference

That, briefly, is the position at the moment. And that is why, when you ask a professor of music "What is the difference between a brass-band and a military band?" he will reply: "It's purely a matter of pitch". Which seems to put the whole thing in a nutshell.

Q. Oh, does it? Why—you haven't said a single word about Silver bands.

A. Not quite true. I have and I haven't.

Q. I don't understand. This chapter is clearly called 'Military Bands, Brass Bands and . . .'

A. Quite so. The explanation is simple. You've just learned something of the furtive, hole-in-the-corner existence of brass-bandsmen all these years?

Q. Yes.

A. Well, it so happens that these fine lads, in the interests of culture, have often defied the law and dared to play in forbidden places. Many's the time a concert has been broken up by the warning cry of "Coppers!" And these martyrs of the music world have been obliged to put their pride in their pockets and their instruments inside their jackets.

Q. I can't see where all this is leading us. All I asked . . .

A. Inside their jackets. Years of doing this has had its effect on most instruments you see. All the pushing in and out of jackets has worn off the brass finish and the instruments have now a shiny, *silvery* appearance.

Q. I've never heard such . . . how on earth can you get a thing like a tuba under your jacket?

A. That's a question you'd better ask a tuba-player. That is, if you can find one. Tuba players are *always* getting caught, poor chaps.

7

Opera

What Is Opera?

"OPERA" IS the plural of "opus", and whichever way you look at it, it can only mean "works". Now we know what happens when an author has a whole lot of articles and stories and things he can't sell; he bribes a publisher to put them all together, throw in a few cute illustrations, and publish the lot under the title of "Miscellany" or "Omnibus" or "The Whisky-Lover's Bedside Book". His motto is, "if you can't tempt 'em, *swamp* 'em!" As with authors, so with composers; all *their* rejected stuff is probably bundled together, too, and given some catchy title like "The One Who Shoots with Magic Bullets" ("Der Freischütz" for short). Instead of an illustrator, they use dress designers, scene painters and librettists. They go the whole hog. When you go to an opera, that's what you get—the works.

Two More Theories

This is about the most logical and coherent explanation you are ever likely to get, but if you are *still* curious there are a couple of other theories you might like to know about:

1. An opera is a play set to music;
2. An opera is music set to a play.

(You see what I mean? You should have been satisfied with the first explanation.)

An Aphorism

The musical world is divided on these two definitions. Librettists are in favour of the first one, but musicians are in the opposite camp. This is natural enough, as their share of the box-office depends on what part of the opera the management reckon is the more important. Some say this, others that. Well, which is? One calls to mind (one doesn't, really; one had to look it up in an encyclopaedia) that well known aphorism which says that *music begins where speech ends.* If you can make any sense out of this, then you're welcome to it. But it's more than likely that you've ceased to care *what* opera is—and that makes two of us. Perhaps we'd better get down to some Hard Facts.

How Opera Came About

Opera was invented one Saturday night, about half past eight, in 1580. It was started by a crowd of Florentine intellectuals and ice-cream merchants who called themselves the *Camerata* (they *had* thought of the *Co-Optimists,* but someone said it'd already been used). According to the experts, what they were really trying to do was to revive the Greek Drama. What usually happens, of course, when you try reviving something that's been dead for a couple of thousand years is that you end up with a bad smell. The Camerata must have known this, and they probably weren't the least bit interested in the past; they were too fond of dabbling in "futures" on 'Change'.

How Opera Houses Came To Be Built

It so happened that the Italians had a particularly bad summer in 1580—all the boarding-houses along the Adriatic coast were practically deserted, and the amusement arcades weren't doing a thing. As a result, the Camerata people found themselves with a whole lot of ice-cream on their hands. The only hope was to try and sell it indoors, and if there'd been such a thing as cinemas in those days that's where they most certainly would have taken it. There weren't, and that's how they came to build opera-houses.

The First Opera

The next thing was, to put on some kind of show—you couldn't have all those people just sitting there in plush seats, eating ice-cream and maybe finding fault with it (it didn't keep so well in those days). The question then arose as to who was going to write this show; this greatly bothered some of the Camerata, because, though they were very intellectual, their literary experience was confined to painting "STOP ME AND BUY ONE" on handcarts. Eventually they tossed up, and two people named Rinuccini and Jacopo Peri lost. They called their joint work "Dafne"; admittedly they couldn't spell very well, but then intellectuals don't necessarily *have* to. This opera was all about this girl who told her mother that a certain hot-blooded god was always following her home from needlework classes. Now lots of girls would give their right arms to be followed home by a hot-blooded god, and perhaps Dafne wasn't complaining at that. But her mother was a bit on the old-fashioned side, and she upped and turned Dafne into a laurel-tree. She'd only ever had one of these in the garden before, and she'd always wanted to call the house "The Laurels". Keeping up with the Joneses is all very well, but on cold winter nights Dafne used to stare in through the living-room windows and wonder if this wasn't taking it a bit far.

Such a simple domestic story, faithfully reflecting the everyday life of the average family, couldn't possibly fail. Of course the Florentines were most enthusiastic about this—the very first opera, and after a few days everyone was going around whistling that beautiful aria, "Trees".

Popularity Of The Aria

"Aria", of course, simply means "air", and the singers of that time used up far more aria than they do today; now they take up more area. The producers soon tumbled to it that it was the singing that drew the crowds. It wasn't so difficult to arrive at this conclusion, because after a while the audience ceased to take any interest in the story, and in between their favourite songs they would play draughts, pontoon and postman's knock. It was round about this time that the "star system" was introduced, and many entertainers were built up into celebrities by advertising . . .

> TOP TENOR CACCINI *SWEARS BY* "Bella Vacca" CREAM CHEESE ! ! !
>
> "For months I was tortured by a powerful desire for sleep" confesses this virtuoso of the larynx, "especially during the night. I was at my wits' end . . . but now, it's all over—thanks to "Bella Vacca". Half a pound will keep me awake for *days*—hurrah for "Bella Vacca"! ! !

Male Sopranos And Their Peculiarities

But most of the singers didn't need any advertising. They were great technicians, and some of the men could sing soprano, which isn't easy—especially in tights. These male sopranos were even more conceited and temperamental than the women—and that's saying something. If a performance wasn't going right they would scream and spit, which gave them an edge on the women as they could spit much further (on a good night Farenelli could make the second row of the balcony). They were just as liable to storm over to one of the cast who might be a little flat and tear out his beard by the roots. Often enough the beard would belong to a female baritone, which made things awkward all round. Things like this were always happening to Farenelli but he was so famous he just didn't care. The king of Spain liked his style so much that he made him sing the same four songs to him every night for ten years, i.e., three thousand, six hundred and fifty times. The three thousand, six hundred and fifty-*first* occasion was an unfortunate one for Farinelli. He went and forgot the words. That was about the time he started singing round the pubs.

Sometimes an opera singer would decide to skip whole

He went and forgot the words

chunks of the script, partly because there was large hot-pot supper going on in the balcony, and partly because it was pretty dull stuff anyway. Either way, he just couldn't wait for his next solo spot, when he could show off with a real tricky bit of vibrato. They had a special kind of singing to cover up the skipped parts, called the *recitativo secco*. They could get through a lot of the plot that way:

> "Then the scene changes to Calabria, where the seven mad monks turn into snakes and the charcoal-burner poisons the general's sister-in-law because she hasn't *really* got the magic handkerchief at all. Meanwhile, the princess has completely forgotten to commit suicide, as she had promised the dwarf, and now she drinks the love potion by mistake. Angrily Urq storms the castle with his men, and in the battle that follows, everyone is killed except Urq, who sings . . . (*Aside*) Enrico! Where's Enrico?"

Indispensability of Bass Player

Enrico, of course, is not in the opera—he is merely the conductor, who has taken advantage of the *recitativo* to slip off and take a hand or two at a pontoon school in one of the boxes. One by one the other musicians have slipped off, too, and only the double-bass player is left (he isn't so keen on indoor games) and for appearance's sake he gives the occasional *plonk* during the *recitativo*.

Aria D'Imitazione

If there were no signs of the orchestra coming back, the singer would very likely do an *aria d'imitazione*. He was usually very good at this, and could imitate, at a moment's notice, birds, frogs, cows, goats and a horseman blowing a hunting-horn while at full gallop. He *had* to—these things were in the script. Eventually some of the stars got a bit above themselves, and refused to do such parts on the grounds that it was "scab" labour. They were so powerful by this time that the producers could do nothing else but engage *real* birds, frogs, cows, goats, and horsemen. This was a bit of a headache, because most horsemen were tone-deaf.

Aria Aggiunta

The imitations were very popular, and by the time the artist had got round to doing Charles Laughton in a scene from "The Mutiny on the Bounty" most of the audience were back in their seats and facing the stage. And once the orchestra were ready, the moment was ripe for the opera-singer's favourite aria—the *aria aggiunta.* Naturally enough, he would occasionally get sick and tired of singing the same old songs about people's tiny hands being frozen and their hearts softly awakening. After all, they were only human (mind you, I wouldn't like anyone to take me up on that). Anyway, once in a while he would walk to the front of the stage with a disarming smile and address the audience . . .

> "Thank you friends, thank you . . . bless you one and all, and that includes you in the attic! (blowing kisses to gallery). And now, if you'll bear with me a moment, I should like to sing you something very special. A new number, straight from Florence, written by my very, very good friends, Dom Cimarosa and Al Ventura. It's called, "Love's a Sweet Little Word" and I'm sure you're gonna like it . . . Right, Enrico?"

He would throw into the pit a bundle of music which poor Enrico had never seen before in his life; the thing about the *aria aggiunta* being that it wasn't in the script. To cover up their lack of practice, the musicians would play very loud, and improvise a bit here and there. The crowd loved a noise, there'd be an encore, everyone would join in, and a good time would be had by all.

8

Going to a Concert

Disturbing Fact About Concert-Going

FOR THE benefit of those who have never been to a concert, it should be explained that the experience is very different from watching a film or a play—in fact there isn't really any comparison. The reason being that at a concert *the lights stay on the whole time*. There are other differences, of course, but this is the one which ought to be emphasized.

Advantages Of Darkness In Cinema

Naturally enough, some newcomers to music find the staying-on of the lights a bit disturbing (I almost said disconcerting, but that would never do). Of course, there are many advantages about being in the darkness at the cinema. If you are feeling tired, you can take a quiet nap; if your feet are feeling tired, you can take your shoes off. If you are feeling wide-awake, but find the film boring, you can leer at the girl in the next seat, safe in the knowledge that she doesn't even know she's being leered at. But the most important advantage is this: if you are fed-up with the whole proceedings you can get up in the middle of the performance and slip quietly away. No-one knows you've gone; no-one cares.

Concert-halls, however, offer none of these facilities. *Once you're in, you're in.* No power on earth can get you out of that seat before the interval, at the very earliest. The management is so keen on your enjoying yourself on their premises that they post a number of vigilant attendants at the exit-doors to make sure you don't get out before you've had your money's worth. You might say that they are sort of "chuckers-out" in reverse, and to get past them you've got to provide a pretty good reason, like dropping dead. Even then it's very likely they'll want to see a death certificate. Chuckers-in at the Albert Hall are still smarting over the memory of the occasion when an elderly admiral, who'd been dragged along by his niece, suddenly keeled over in the middle of the Stravinsky. Sympathetically they made way for the stretcher, but as soon as it had passed them the admiral jumped off, shouted "Every man for himself!" and leaped into a passing taxi.

Drawbacks Of Not Having A Programme

Another reason why the lights are left on is to enable you to read the programme, the cost of which you probably hadn't bargained for. *But buy one you must.* Those who are too mean to do so are very easy to spot; they twitch uncomfortably in their seats as they wait for the programme to start (they can't even light a cigarette, of course). And when it does start, they have to sit there all evening, listening to a whole lot of music without knowing what key it's in. Or even, for that matter, what the thing is called. (Conductors never say, between items, "And now, ladies and gents, I hope you'll enjoy our interpretation of that old favourite, Sibelius' "Voces Intimae, Opus 56 . . ."). They don't know, either, that Baldoni's Famous Ices will be on sale during the interval. Their ignorance, in short, verges on the pathetic.

You with your programme, however, are sitting pretty. You learn right away that the first item is to be the Overture from Bignelli's opera, "The Squinting Peacock". You know when he wrote it, how many minutes it takes, and what comes afterwards; all in all, you feel rather sorry for the big, bald man in front, who has no programme and sits biting his nails. There's a whole mine of information about the piece that you have and he hasn't. How nice it is, for instance, to know that

"The overture opens with a fortissimo chord, followed by the first subject stated, animato, by the woodwind."

That seems fair enough; nothing like the old "fortissimo" to get things started with a bang; and it will be quite interesting to try and locate the woodwind on that little plan of the orchestra that you have—ready for the moment that they go into action. Then what?

"The theme is repeated by the strings, then by the brass . . ."

(Copycats! Still, it's all in fun.)

"and in this way they proceed to the allegro deciso con impeto."

Do they, indeed? Still there's nothing here that a couple of weeks at San Remo won't cure.

"This brilliantly outlines the gay, quixotic character of the incorrigible Gobbolio . . ."

Just a minute—Gobbolio? Who is Gobbolio and how did *he* get in here? But there's more to come, and the next few lines might tell us something about him . . .

"Then comes a larghetto (F Ma 3/4) on the lugubrious lament, 'Il Mio Naso E Lungo Quasi Un Metro', to which is added an aggressive allegro—which in turn leads to a theme in F Sharp Ma (2/2), ingeniously diverging to another . . ."

At this point you undergo a sudden, inexplicable bout of dizziness, and the words start swimming before your eyes. Gobbolio doesn't seem to matter any more, and you find yourself looking hard at the big, bald man in front. He has stopped biting his nails, and is sitting back—arms folded,

Tap him sharply on the shoulder

One Way Of Dealing With Your Programme

eyes closed, with a placid smile on his face. Somehow you don't feel sorry for him now—in fact, you find him rather irritating. There's only one thing to do, of course: tap him sharply on the shoulder, then when he turns round, shove your programme into his hand.

That should teach him manners, if nothing else; whoever heard of anyone *smiling* during a concert?

Perhaps it isn't surprising that a Growing Body of Opinion (there's my brother and myself, for a start) is demanding that the whole business of programmes and programme notes be investigated, with a view to some drastic reforms. All that stuff we've been looking at is very clever and all that, but is it serving its proper purpose? Does it, in fact, tell us *what we want to know*? (That is, of course, providing that we want to know anything. Some of us don't and it doesn't seem to do us any harm.)

When you think about it, it shouldn't be so very difficult

to produce a programme that provides a wealth of really useful information—especially to the newcomer to the concert-hall. Of course it would have to be rather different from the conventional thing; it would have to be written in plain, straightforward English, for a start. It could begin with a sort of friendly welcome:

"Well, friend—here you are! And here you'll jolly well have to stay for the next couple of hours—you'd better get that in your head for a start. During that time you will be entertained, for want of a better word, by those people in baggy dress suits who are now talking animatedly on the platform. They are probably talking about you—you will have noticed a couple of them sneering in your direction.

"Soon their boss will appear, and he's easy to spot because his trousers are twice as baggy as the others—and that's saying something. When he gives the signal, all those musicians will begin blowing, banging and scraping for the good of your soul. And, as there's no escape (incidentally, did you know there was rather a snazzy revue on at the Coliseum tonight? There's always tomorrow, of course) the very least you can do is to behave yourself and try and do the right thing . . .

"This symphony thing, for instance. You'll see that it has four 'movements', each with a different name—allegro moderato, adagio sostenuto, scherzo and allegro scherzando. *Take no notice of these names*. You will soon learn that every movement sounds exactly the same. All you need remember is that the symphony is in four bits—but MARK THIS: *It's more than your life's worth to start clapping between any two of these bits*. Everyone will look daggers, one or two old ladies will click their tongues, and possibly one of the chuckers-in will clamp a heavy hand on your shoulder. You will appreciate, if this is your first visit to a concert, that you've really got yourself into something.

"The first bit—the allegro whats-its-name—lasts for 6 minutes, the second bit 7, the third 9, and the fourth, blimey, that goes on for ever! There's no smoking, of course, but there's one consolation; you can help yourself to a soft-centre . . . provided that you do it at a time when you won't be heard. An appropriate moment this evening, for instance, would be three-quarters of the way through the second movement. The orchestra kicks up such a din at that point that you could eat soup and no-one would hear you doing it.

"IMPORTANT WARNING: There's no use carefully refraining from clapping all the way through this symphony, then ruining everything by doing it too soon at the end. And this may well happen. There's what you might call a *Phoney Finale* before you come to the real one—about two minutes before, in fact. Hold your applause until you see *at least twelve other people clapping first*.

"DON'T applaud too long, otherwise you'll be last down the aisle when the interval starts. Gents' cloaks to the left, foyer to the right. Incidentally, steer clear of Baldoni's Ices—all that stuff on the back page about 'the Delicacy for the Discriminating' is *sheer rubbish*. If you want to know the truth, Baldoni's Ices have a marked flavour of carbolic.

"If you're *really* dry (and you *are*, aren't you?) they sell a particularly luscious bitter over at Rooney's Free House (opposite the side entrance). If the commissionaire *with the drooping grey moustache* is on duty you're in luck; press a silver coin into his hand and he'll thoughtfully look the other way. If he isn't, then getting out is largely a question of individual courage and initiative.

"Once having got to Rooney's, you'd be wise to *stay there till closing-time*, because the second half of this programme is even worse than the first . . .

"Now then, you others, how are you on ballet music?

Wait till you hear about this lot . . ."

Applause

You will have noticed that the new kind of programme notes have some important things to say about clapping in the right parts. But it's not enough to know *when* to applaud—you should also learn *how* to, which is far more difficult.

It all starts, oddly enough, well before the programme itself. And how it comes about is this: You'll find that at every concert you attend, without exception, there's always one musician who turns up late—far later than everyone else. For some reason it always seems to be a violinist (perhaps their hair takes a lot longer to comb than the others, they certainly have more per head). Anyway, when he comes slinking on to the platform, trying to look casual, it's sort of traditional that the audience let him know that he hasn't got away with it—not by a long chalk.

Ironical Applause

Everyone in the audience exchanges sly grins, then they start up what might be called Ironical Applause. This is much the same as ordinary applause so far as the clapping is concerned; the difference being that you should have a faint smile playing at the corners of your mouth. Some people have been to so many concerts that they have perpetual smiles playing at the corners of their mouths (it hurts, too). If the subtlety of the thing still hasn't got over to you, try and recall the kind of noise the spectators make when a crack centre-forward fluffs a penalty for the visiting side.

Warm-Hearted Applause

Generally speaking, your applause should get more enthusiastic as the evening goes on, reaching a sort of crescendo when the celebrity soloist makes his appearance. The effect to aim at here is Warm-Hearted Applause. This is particularly important, since the celebrity is, more often than not, a foreigner, and the idea is the audience should let him know that he's welcome; they appreciate that he is, so to speak, playing away and they are ready to make allowances for breaking strings, accidents with the piano-stool, and so on.

Care should be taken, however, not to let the emotion of the occasion run away with you. Whistling with two fingers in your mouth and shouting "Good old 'Arry" won't do you the least bit of good—or 'Arry either. This, of course, does not apply to Promenade Concerts. You can get away with just about anything at Promenade Concerts—a fact not always appreciated by those who are attending one for the first time. The lady, for example, who wrote to the "Times" complaining that the uncouth man next to her had jumped up in the middle of a scherzo and shouted "Go on—moider the bum!" just didn't understand. The gentleman was probably pointing out, admittedly in a sarcastic kind of way, that Mendelssohn's work was not being interpreted in the way that he (Mendelssohn) had intended.

The importance of not clapping in between movements has already been stressed, but it isn't always so easy as it sounds. It takes a pretty strong will at times. After a while you will have noticed that a lot of the string section can't wait for the end of a movement so that they can start tuning their instruments furiously; they seem to enjoy this better than playing. Then the time is bound to come when you are caught out; a movement ends, and all the violinists sit staring like statues, not tuning up or anything. Just as you start smiting your silly great hands together, they turn and grin at one another: "Got him that time!"

Danger Of Not Clapping At All

If you follow your programme properly, of course, this won't happen to you. Neither are you likely to commit an even worse offence—that of *not* clapping when you ought to. There was a very unhappy affair once at Carnegie Hall; it happened during the printers' strike of 1936 (someone is going to say that they don't remember any printers' strike in 1936. Of course they don't. It wasn't in the papers). Anyway on account of the strike there were no programmes at this concert, which was being conducted by a Celebrity from

Europe. Naturally, no-one in the audience knew how many movements there were; they didn't even know how many items were coming up. They were in a bit of a quandary, and everyone decided not to clap until someone else started. *Everybody*. After about an hour-and-a-half of complete silence, the conductor's nerve broke. He threw down his baton and cried. He said he'd never been so insulted, and if he'd thought they were going to be like *that* he'd never have come. What's more he'd never set foot in that hall again as long as his name was Otto Wurzenspiel. His name *wasn't* Otto Wurzenspiel, and he was back again a fortnight after. This time he had a large card under his jacket which he kept pulling out after each item. It said, NOW YOU MAY CLAP, but it didn't make the slightest difference. It wasn't till he got back to Europe that he realized he'd gone and written the notice in his native tongue, which was Serbo-Croat, a language that a lot of people aren't very strong on. Well, you can't think of *everything* . . .

The Interval

Another tricky period for the newcomer to the concert-hall is the interval. At a football-match you can cheerfully slander everyone in sight, or stamp your feet in time to the canned music; but here your only relaxation is to cross the foyer for a coffee. You are quite free to talk, but you'll find difficulty in saying something that doesn't sound either stupid or out-of-place . . . ("Marvellous orchestra, isn't it?" "Typically Russian, what?" "I must get this waistcoat cleaned.") If you observe the hardened concert-goers, you'll notice that they've learned the art of saying nothing with great authority. The thing is to *look* as though you're having an intellectual discussion.

Following A Score

You would be wise not to start the practice of following a concert with the score on your knees until you have found your feet, as it were. This may sound awfully pedantic, but try to ensure that the score you bring *has some connection with the programme being played on that particular evening.* Then again, unless you know what it's all about, it's probable that you won't know when to turn over. That's all right, you may say, you'll just wait for that fellow with the monocle next to you. But the chances are, *he's* waiting for *you* to turn over, and you might still be staring intelligently at Page One while everyone is clapping and shouting "Encore!"

Difficulty In Making An Impression

If it happens that you *are* able to read a score (if so, then why aren't you on the platform? Come to that, why are you reading this book?) you'll find it difficult, not to say impossible, to persuade all the people around you that you are cleverer than they are (they've probably had that character with the

" . . . *look* as though you're having an intellectual discussion."

monocle weighed up for a long time). You might say that it gives you some kind of aesthetic satisfaction, if you know what that means (and if you do, this *definitely* isn't your book). Let us suppose, for argument's sake, that you have discovered that the leader of the violins has inadvertently played a bit that ought to have been played by the 'cellos. Just what can you do about it? If the same kind of thing happened at a football match, you could jump up and shout "Foul!" or "Take 'Im Orff!" All you can do at a concert, however, is to mutter, *sotto voce,* "Dear, dear!" or, if it happens to be a very loud piece, "Tut, tut!" This kind of thing is very inhibiting artistically; it also makes you feel a bit of a Charlie.

Using Score For Fun And Education

This is not to say that a score doesn't have its uses. The next time you take one along with you to a concert, have a good look at it. You'll see that on every page there are lots of lines with little round things scattered all over them. These round things are called *NOTES* (stop me if I'm getting too technical) and the *hollow* round things are called *MINIMS* or *SEMIBREVES* (these are the big, fat ones). If the concert is beginning to get you down, you try getting out your pencil and filling all the hollow notes till they look like *CROTCHETS* or *QUAVERS*.

It's *ever* such fun. And there's this about it, too: it *does* help to take your mind off the music.

9

Critics

THE PRACTICE of musical criticism is as old as music itself, dating back to the palaeolithic era we were talking about earlier on. In those days, of course, it was a bit on the vicious side, though, come to think of it, it hasn't changed all that much. If the star drummer of the tribe was a little off form—a touch of nervous indigestion, perhaps—and he inadvertently *boomed* when he should have given a mere *bonk*, then he was sure to be slated by the critics. This kind of experience inevitably left its mark on the artists, as the critics used pretty heavy slates.

Primitive Critics

Today our critics seldom resort to violence, though they can sometimes be seen pulling tongues at mezzo-sopranos during the interval. On the other hand, they are allowed to say pretty much what they like, and they get paid a steady salary for doing it; which puts them practically on a par with the Prime Minister and the Archbishop of Canterbury. All critics are nasty, the only difference being that some are worse than others. The degree of nastiness depends largely on which School of Criticism they subscribe to. (Incidentally this is about the only thing they ever do subscribe to; their lives

Modern Critics

are largely one long round of free passes, free meals and free drinks.)

Critics As People

Critics can be divided roughly into two main groups, and you might say, therefore, that there are two main schools of criticism (no-one would argue if you did). By examining these people carefully (background, philosophy, blood-group and so on) we should be able to get a much firmer grasp on the Contemporary Musical Scene (I'm not too sure about that last bit, but it looks rather good with capitals). We shall call them A and B.

Critic A knows nothing whatever about music, *knows* he knows nothing about it, yet *has no rooted objection to it* . . . it doesn't give him headaches or anything like that.

Critic B, on the other hand, knows *everything* about music, but *hates the sight and sound of everyone and everything connected with it.*

The Type Who Knows Nothing

In spite of a tendency to become absent-minded when it's his turn to buy a round of drinks, A is not particularly anti-social; in fact he may be comparatively harmless. He has drifted into this profession for any one of a variety of reasons. He may have been lucky enough to have been born with a double-barrelled name and a string of imposing-looking initials. He may possess those long skinny hands, peculiar to people who have never done a day's work in their lives, which his mother at one time thought were "artistic". It could be that he got himself transferred from the post of Lobby Correspondent because sitting in concert-halls seemed cushier (less draughty, too). But the most likely reason, editors being what they are, is that the boss has had an eye on him ever since the night he fixed the Press Club piano after someone had poured a lot of beer inside it.

Once appointed, he grows his hair long, sports a beard and wears a floppy bow-tie. It's not that he's affected—it's just that he's conscientious enough to want to look the part.

How To Spot Him In A Crowd

In the concert season you might see him in a maroon velour hat with a cape thrown casually across his shoulders. If you look closely, however, you'll see that it's really a *cycling* cape; the more he uses his bike, the more he makes on expenses.

So far as he is concerned, the subject of music should never be discussed in the presence of ladies; in fact it should be avoided altogether if possible. His argument that it's bad enough having to *listen* to music all the time without having to *write* about it as well is an interesting one. And it gives him a lot of scope, because there are so many other things he *can* write about—the blotchy printing on the programmes for a start.

There are, however, three serious subjects which he dwells on fairly regularly, just to show he takes his profession seriously. These are

(a) Members of the audience,
(b) Members of the orchestra, and
(c) The composer of the main work.

Attitude To Audience

It's a strange thing, but both critics A and B have the same opinion about the audience (i.e., the people who keep them in a job). So far as they are concerned, these people are lower than the bottom note on a double-bass—they just can't do a thing right. If they roll up in their thousands to hear something they like, then they're for it. The programme that attracted them ("popular"—ugh!) is, it seems, absolutely awful, and no true music-lover could even look at it without feeling sick. If, however, everyone stays away from a concert because they don't like what's on (a pretty lame excuse, admittedly) then A throws up his hands in despair and wonders what the world is coming to.

Sometimes the audience turn up in moderate numbers, neither too large nor too small, and you'd think that he couldn't say much about that. You'd be wrong . . .

"The overture, alas, was utterly ruined by the noisy

entrance of late-comers. Surely these music-lovers (!) can make an occasional effort to arrive just a few minutes earlier? We are well aware of the shortcomings of the public transport systems, but there *are* other modes of travel. Some of us are not too proud to pedal our way to the concert-hall in order to bask in the music of the masters . . ."

If there are no late-comers, as sometimes happens, A still has a card up his sleeve . . .

"Frankly, I could tell you more about Sprodka's Violin Concerto (Note: He couldn't, you know!) if it hadn't been effectively drowned by all that coughing. Why people choose such dramatic moments to cough is quite beyond me. Could it be that they are *bored* by Sprodka? If so, then these barking philistines had better save their croaks for the music-hall, where they belong."

It's no secret that A, in fact, spends his night off in that very way—going to the music-hall. His wife says that if he didn't get away from that highbrow stuff once in a while he'd go crazy.

Attitude To The Orchestra

When it comes to the orchestra, A is much more polite. There is a streak of honesty in him, somewhere, that will make him admit, when tipsy, that the average musician does know more about music than he does. As a result, he tries to keep on good terms with him; and in order to pick up any pleasant bits of gossip he hangs around the bars and pawn-shops of the Bohemian quarter during the day. He is often rewarded, too . . .

"During the enchanting 'Romeo and Juliet' last night, one was aware that Dawn Scattergood's fingers fluttered across her harp-strings with a new exuberance—and little wonder! For Dawn's little secret had leaked out just before the concert began . . . the secret of her *pianissimo* wedding last week-end. And the lucky man? None other than Philharmonic favourite, trombonist George Duggs, and

I'm sure we all wish them many years of sweet harmony! Incidentally, it is whispered that Henry Schreiner relinquishes the leader's chair next month to start a fish business in Hampstead. It seems only . . ."

Culture Rears Its Head

So far, A's pieces have been fairly straightforward. Simple off-the-cuff stuff. Every now and then, however, his editor has a sort of Culture-drive to appease someone on the board. "This music column", he announces, "will have to have a bit more meat in it. If necessary, you'll have to get hold of some facts, such as, say, what's being played and who wrote it . . ." A kindly smile, then, quietly: "I'm sorry, old chap—it's a rough assignment—but then that's Fleet Street . . ."

A drinks two thoughtful whiskies, and eventually decides to write something about the composer of the main work for that evening. Such a project is no light one, involving at least an hour in the public library. In fact, sometimes it takes a lot longer, as most composers' names are hard to find in the indexes because of the way they are spelt. To find Chaikovsky, for instance, you have to look under "T". Vorak, on the other hand is found among the "D's" (and what's more there's something gone seriously wrong with the middle of that word).

Advertising The Composer

Once he's got the name he wants, our critic delves pretty deep, and by the time he leaves the library he's feeling very pleased with himself—bursting with Culture, as you might say. So elated does he feel, that he's eager to show off his newly-acquired knowledge not only to the editor, but to the whole literate world. And to introduce his next column, nothing but the largest possible headlines will do . . .

KNICKERBOCKERED GENIUS WROTE
MASTERPIECE IN
BLACKCURRANT
JAM!

This, of course, is an excellent example of how to catch the reader's eye, bearing in mind the wide variety of people, all with different interests, who read his paper. Seeing the headline, the musically-inclined will immediately wonder—*which* genius and *which* masterpiece? The housewife wonders, why *blackcurrant* jam? And everyone else wonders, what the hell? It's got them all guessing, and they can't help but read on:

"While listening last evening to Schulberg's brilliant and memorable 'Wasp' Suite, I looked round at the enthralled listeners, and wondered how many of them—if any—were aware of the dramatic way in which it was born. It was during a family picnic in the Black Forest that young Jacob Schulberg, then only seven years old, suddenly exclaimed: 'Papa—I have to tell you that there is a wasp reclining on your nose.' 'Never mind, my son', smiled his father, 'for soon it will go away . . . that is the way of things.' But the boy only frowned. 'No', he protested, 'It must not go away—it must remain still, while I compose a Suite about it.' 'Yes, yes', said the old man gently, 'But not just now, surely? You have no pencil or paper with you.' Whereupon the budding genius, undaunted, smoothed out the tablecloth on the grass and said quietly: 'Mama, please pass the blackcurrant jam . . .' "

The Second Critic

Critic B hasn't much time for his rival, which isn't so surprising really, as he hasn't much time for anyone. Any drinking he does is done alone at the end of the bar (which means that at least he has to pay for it). At the core he is a frustrated genius who never made the grade through no fault of his own. He will tell you that as a boy he was on the way to becoming another Kreisler, till one day a great catastrophe befell him and blighted his career. He will show you his right hand and demonstrate the restricted action of his skinny fingers. And all because of that fool in the cinema who brought his big foot down just as he was groping for a dropped aniseed-ball . . .

Boy genius undaunted

What He *Looks Like*

He doesn't look a bit like A. He has one of those scrubby chins that can't make its mind up whether it's growing a beard or not. His evening ensemble is quite informal (and that's putting it mild). It usually consists of, say, a brown striped jacket that contrasts nicely with blue melton trousers and army-grey socks. He doesn't dress awfully well; the truth is, he's still rather cut-up over not being a violin virtuoso, not to mention losing his aniseed-ball, and he just doesn't care.

The audience are so far beneath his contempt that he just doesn't waste a single word on them; they may not be there at all so far as he is concerned. He objects to every programme on principle, but it is the musicians who really feel the lash of his words. All his bitterness comes out (wouldn't you think his parents would have made him take up fretwork or something?) as he proceeds to flay the instrumentalists one by one. Any pianinst who ventures into the same hall as him would be well advised to make some excuse and slip off home before the concerto. Otherwise he is certainly due to be condemned as "shaky" or "pitifully lacking in confidence". Naturally! Wouldn't anyone feel shaky with *him* scowling down there in the front row? And if there's anything likely to destroy a man's confidence, it's the sight of a brown striped jacket worn with blue melton trousers and army-grey socks. When there's no pianist, then the violin section are most likely to be attacked; he's always accusing them of not playing together, and he refers to them as being "ragged" (*he* should talk!). Unlike the solitary pianist, however, they usually remain unperturbed; their view is that there are so many of them that he'll never know which are the guilty ones who are out of step, so to speak. Heaven help them if he ever does.

Why Cellos Buzz

Another thing that makes him see red is what he terms "buzzing" from the 'cellos. No-one else ever seems to bother about this, and in any case it's important to remember the

"Sometimes they get frustrated not to say bored stiff"

'cellists' point of view. Night after night they have to sit behind the violins and listen to them playing all the tunes that everyone knows; while they have to scrape out low-pitched twiddly bits that only seem to get in the way. Naturally they get frustrated, not to say bored stiff. You can well imagine the leader leaning over to his deputy during a particularly dull symphony and talking out of the corner of his mouth . . .

"How's it going, Spike?

"Browned off, Nobby. Here—you know that French horse the commissionaire gave me for today's race?"

"Ah?"

"Just another stiff—way down the course it finished. That's three quid down the drain this week."

"A great life if you don't weaken. Tell you what though, Spike . . ."

"What, Nobby?"

"Bet you can't make a noise like a bumble-bee."

"Bet you I can . . ."

And the next thing you know, there they both are, buzzing away like mad, with all their fellow-'cellos following suit. A lot of people reckon it makes a jolly interesting sound, too —but not B.

The French Horn Mystery

Considering his background, it isn't surprising that he harbours a grudge against the strings of the orchestra. However, there is yet another instrumentalist who lives in dread of him, and that is the French horn player. This critic will often sit through a whole concert, ignoring everyone else, just for the satisfaction of hearing the unfortunate man drop a note or two; this, in his opinion, is worth a whole vitriolic column. Unfortunately, he is rewarded all too often. What usually happens is this . . .

Somewhere in the score, all the strings have to play, in unison, a certain phrase. It might be

Grapes with hairs on?

At this point they stop, and the French horn is supposed to answer promptly

Goose-gogs!

"I always considered myself a virtuoso"

Now it is a very sad thing, but about seven times out of ten the poor man blows hard but *nothing comes out*. Not so much as half a goose-gog.

It's an experience that happens to the most accomplished of horn-players, and none of them have ever been able to give a proper explanation. One eminent musician was once questioned after a particularly ghastly silence in the middle of Dvorak's "New World" Symphony.

Eminent Musician's Despair

"I cannot understand eet," he said, choking with sobs (he was a foreigner, which will indicate that he was *really* eminent). "I always considered myself a virtuoso, 'aving studied at Rome, Paris, and Crewe. Everything I did was correct, and when it left me that note was in perfect condition. So far as I am concerned eet ees the Marie Celeste business all over again . . ."

The Fungus Theory

All kinds of theories have been put forward as to what happens to all those notes that are never heard of again. Probably the most interesting one is that after the instrument reaches a certain age some kind of weird fungus starts growing somewhere in the heart of it; in the depths of its arterial system, so to speak. This fungus has to breathe, same as everyone else, and every now and then it so happens that as the musician is playing—i.e., breathing *out*, chance has it that the fungus is breathing *in*. In this way the note is sort of neutralized, and nothing happens. When such absorbing theories are put to critic B, he is inclined to sneer. He will tell you that he has tried sawing an offending French horn in half and found nothing there. He doesn't realize that this particular species of fungus would probably disintegrate when exposed to the daylight; otherwise why does it choose to live in the middle of a French horn?

Sometimes he can be quite obtuse, and a lot of people are beginning to wonder if he really is the expert he is cracked up to be.

New Angles On Criticism

About once a year, usually round about August, something seems to happen to the music column. This is because A (or B) is on holiday, and instead of the usual stuff you may find yourself reading something like this:

". . . Once more the brasses were on the attack—the rest

after the last round seemed to have given them a much-needed shot in the arm. The trombones were punching away like pistons, in out, in out, and two thousand excited fans wondered just how long they could keep up the pace. But the fiddles weren't played out yet. For the next two rounds they were on the defensive, cool, calm and well-drilled, as they waited for an opening. When it came, whoosh!—in they swept, full pelt, and next minute, believe it or not, it was the brass boys who were on the retreat! Ye gods—those strings had guts . . ."

Apart from an unfortunate tendency to refer to movements as "rounds", the sports editor is often so enthusiastic about the referee's (i.e., the conductor's) brilliant footwork, which gets him reminiscing about Spider Llewellyn of Swansea, that he quite forgets about the orchestra altogether. After all this excitement, it's quite a relief to read the efforts of Miss Susannah Thimble when *her* turn comes:

. . . "Sitting behind Mrs. Lorden-Bullock, I spotted that indomitable concert-goer, Lady Swelling, looking very gay and Spanish in a flamenco skirt of black taffeta with a blue sapphire satin top. The high band of sequin embroidery added to the gaiety of the ensemble, and I thought it was an awfully nice gesture on the part of the conductor to get his boys to start off the concert with some kind of Spanish music, with castanets and things. By the way, just back from Majorca is charming sun-tanned Babette Fflemming, who tells me . . ."

It occasionally happens that they have all chosen the same fortnight to go on holiday—the regular music critic, the sports editor, and Susannah Thimble (incidentally, there is no love lost between Miss Thimble and the other two, so you can put *that* idea out of your head). However, in the best traditions of Fleet Street, the music column goes on . . .

"Last night at the Sivic Hall, the Royal Filharmonic

The Model Critic

Orchestra played the Barber of Saville Overture, Lists Hungarian Raphsody, some Strowse Waltzes, and Brahm's 4th Symfony."

This, of course, is criticism at its very best—crisp, truthful and unbiassed, and free from affectation and animosity. The fact is that when it comes to artistic integrity, the office boy is the music critic par excellence.

10

Jazz

THE WORD "jazz" spelt backwards is "zzaj" and that's about the only positive thing we can say about it. Actually, it derives from another word which is never mentioned in the best circles. No-one knows exactly what that word is (or if they do, they aren't saying anything). *Derivation Of Jazz*

In spite of what you may hear, jazz isn't so *very* different from what's known as "straight" music; it is played on the same kind of instrument, like the piano, double bass, drums, clarinet, trumpet and trombone. The only odd man out, as it were, is the saxophone: it takes a very, very clever musician to play anything other than jazz on the saxophone. Many, in fact, won't even try. How, they argue, can anyone be seriously expected to get "straight" music out of a bent instrument? One can't help but sympathize with this realistic point of view. *Similarity To "Straight" Music*

The difference between the two types of music was originally a physical one. Ordinary bands used to perform in *static* places, such as the theatre-pit, the band-stand, or the concert-hall. The musicians just sat down, made themselves comfortable, winked at one or two girls in the audience, adjusted their music, and got cracking. Their performances were level and consistent, and the only things that affected *"Straight" Playing* their tone or technique were warts, the D.T.s, and earthquakes, in that order.

Persecution Of Jazz Musicians

Jazz bands, however, worked under very different conditions. At the start, the tunes they played were regarded as vulgar (as a matter of fact they *were*). Although people may

Jazz. They had to keep moving pretty smartly

have liked them in private, in public they never failed to express their disapproval. That is to say, they used to throw things. And if the players wished to avoid injury, they had to keep moving pretty smartly. Sometimes they marched briskly through the streets as they played, sometimes they found it safer to ride in a covered wagon. The best hiding place of all, though, was on one of the ferry boats that used to sail up and down the Mississippi. If things got really rough they could always batten down the hatches or lower the boats.

Basic Elements

What with all the jogging about (even the steamboats weren't always so steady) the music that came out was far from being straight. As a matter of fact, it was distinctly *wobbly*, and playing from music was out of the question whether you could read music or not. And so we come to the two basic elements of jazz:

1. The distinctive Wobbly technique; and
2. The complete disregard for written notes.

Early Difficul-ties

But there were other difficulties that the pioneers of jazz had to overcome. Things used to get so rowdy on feast days, such as Mardi Gras, that not one but *several* bands used to find themselves huddled together on the same wagon or steamboat. There they all were, cheek by jowl, looking, as an eye-witness puts it, like a Roman phalanx on the retreat (you'd think that all the eye-witnesses of Roman phalanxes had passed on, but there you are).

"Riffs"

The musicians felt comparatively safe like this, and went on playing defiantly. It wasn't very easy, however, playing with someone jogging your elbow the whole time. The trombonist had a particularly tricky problem on his hands, and often he would have to have half-a-dozen goes at one phrase before he could get it right. If you listen to any old jazz record, you can hear those repetitive phrases for yourself. They are called "riffs", from a word which is an absolute shocker.

"Boogie-Woogie"

The pianist was frequently crowded out, too; his right hand could fend for itself, but so far as the bottom half of the keyboard was concerned, he was likely to find that he could only get at three or four notes at a time. He did the best he could with those that were available, and in this way a new style of playing arose, known as "boogie-woogie" (the word that *this* comes from is worse than the other two put together, so you can imagine: musicians must have mixed with some awful company in those days).

Jazz Grows Up

Eventually, however, the inevitable happened, as it usually does. After hearing this music continually for years, day in, day out, it began to grow on people. Soon they began to look down on "straight" music, which they now thought was dull, insipid, and old-fashioned. A lot of re-thinking was done, and gradually jazz found itself becoming respectable. All the brothels and gin-shops began hiring pianists for their establishments (just how respectable can you get?). You might have thought that this would have killed jazz: that playing in a static, sitting-down position would have knocked all the essential wobbliness out of their playing. But not a bit of it. The gin was so strong and the hostesses were so shapely that the pianists, in their tight new evening outfits, were producing music that was *absolutely the last word in wobbliness*. They just couldn't go wrong (not until after the show, anyway).

Piano-Players

It's not surprising that all the pianists of this period were Characters. They smoked big cigars, sported jewelled rings and gold teeth (sometimes it might be the other way about) and always wore their trousers at half-mast as a symbol of the passing of "straight" music. They were all called James P. Johnston or Jelly Roll Morton. (This is a generalization, of course; obviously there were some who did not have either of these names, and *they* were all known as Pinetop Smith.)

What Should They Call It?

By this time they had grown tired of all the rude words that had been creeping into jazz terminology; they felt there was a faint possibility of their profession getting a bad name. So someone organized a large meeting of musicians, arranging bail and parole where necessary, and it was unanimously agreed that it was time their music had a nicer name. Eventually they settled on *Rag-Time*, which they thought had a solid, faintly British-public-school sound about it (actually the man who had suggested it had been reading "Tom Brown's Schooldays" in gaol).

Dancing To Jazz

Spurred on by the success of the new title, they gave fine, dignified names to the rhythms they played. Names like "drag", "crawl", "roll", "shuffle" and "stomp". The new dances made big demands on the dancers, who found dragging, crawling, rolling, and so on, very hard work. But they liked it, and it soon grew into a fierce craze. Everyone wished they could shimmy like their sister Kate. Managements of various establishments found it necessary to increase their dancing space to as much as ten or twelve feet square, and it was still a bit crowded.

Dancers And "Hot Breaks"

One of the biggest and most popular places for dancing was Longshoreman's Hall in New Orleans. It was here, one carnival day in 1902, that a lot of dancers got so carried away that they danced right through the windows, forgetting they were on the second floor; most of them broke their legs, but fortunately there were no longshoremen amongst them.

Those were the days, all right. They don't seem to have dances like that any more.

Why New Orleans?

You will have noticed that the name of New Orleans keeps cropping up when jazz is being discussed. A strange thing, you may think, that of all the places in the world, jazz should be associated with one city. Why New Orleans? you may ask. Why not Washington, Dublin, or Chelsea? According to the experts, the answer lay in the special *atmosphere* of the place (as a matter of fact, the drains *weren't* so good, though that's not what the experts are driving at).

Lay-Out Of New Orleans

They will show you a map of Storeyville, New Orleans, and ask you to see for yourself what an unusual place it was. Just take a look at that map, now (mind the children don't see it, though). Apart from a dozen or so cemeteries, about three-quarters of the city is taken up with saloons, cribs, honky tonks, pawnshops, prisons, and Maisons (your French dictionary will tell you that "maison" means "house", but don't let that fool you). There are also one or two terrace houses just off Rampart Street where apparently people just *lived*. In other words, it's hard to find anything remarkable about the place. You might just as well be looking at a plan of Glasgow, or any common or garden city, and as like as not you are still asking, Why New Orleans? (I hope you are, because there's an interesting theory coming up.)

Source Of Jazz Titles

All this sociological stuff only has the effect of cluttering up your mind. The thing to do is to forget about the experts, and look at the beginnings of jazz calmly and objectively. What are the *pioneer* songs, the evergreens, the classics? Apart from "Way Down Yonder in New Orleans" there are songs about Basin Street, Beale Street, Rampart Street, and St. Louis. I have made searching enquiries, and there are *no such localities* in big towns like Washington, Dublin and Chelsea. None of these songs would, therefore, be likely to go down well with the citizens of those particular towns.

Astonishing Fact About New Orleans

When it comes to New Orleans, however, it's another story. I know it sounds fantastic, but it so happens that New Orleans *contains districts bearing every one of these place names!* (Fate certainly works in strange ways, doesn't it?) Obviously the Louisiana city was the place to launch jazz, and though it's played all over the world now, no-one's in any doubt as to where the blame lies. If someone had had the foresight to write a jazz classic about Washington ("White House Shake") or Dublin ("O'Connell Street Stagger") or Chelsea ("Pensioners Parade") then history might have taken a different turn and World War II might have been averted.

Relation Of Jazz With People

As it was, the impact of jazz on the world was unprecedented. Not only that, nothing like it had ever happened before. The reason lay in its *special appeal*. For a long time people had been complaining about the artificiality of classical music. It was a thing of the past, they alleged, not related to *themselves*. They wanted something that dealt with *everyday* things, that reflected *their own personalities*. Jazz promptly supplied the want with pieces like "Yellow Dog", "Jackass Blues", "Black Bottom Stomp" and "Bucket Got A Hole In it".

Folk music, that's what jazz is. Well, you know what there's nowt so queer as, don't you?

The Blues—Who Started It?

The fact that the Blues are associated with New Orleans doesn't really mean that they started there. Actually they go back for centuries, because people didn't start being miserable at any particular time. However the blues *as we know it* was very first sung in 1173 by a man named Daffydd Gryffyth in a pub just outside Aberystwyth. It seems he had just been stood up on a date, and was sitting in the bar-parlour, moodily strumming his penillion harp. The words just seemed to come to him spontaneously, and they went something like this:

So I stood at the corner, jes' waitin' for my Megan fach . .

Birth and Death Of The Blues

As he elaborated on the theme, quite an audience gathered and no-one noticed when Daffydd's wife came in. Her name *wasn't* Megan, and she wasn't *fach* either—in fact she was rather well-made, and it didn't take her long to wrap the harp round her husband's neck. Daffydd had the blues on and off for most of his life after that, but he never sang again.

Scarlatti Nearly Had Blues

The blues very nearly burst on the world again in 1725, but in different circumstances. Domenico Scarlatti wasn't a bit broody by nature—and he had nothing to be miserable about, either, what with his music selling well and his girls turning up punctually for dates. It just happened that he was having his lunch in the studio when Bruno the cat came in out of the rain. Before he could do a thing about it, it had jumped up on the table, muddy paws and all, and walked right across a blank manuscript page. Scarlatti looked at the blobs on the staff and swore; but a young red-head, who happened to be sitting on his knee at the time, said teasingly: "Go on, Dom—try it on your old harpsichord . . ." Scarlatti would try anything once, and he sat down and played the blobs:

Time Not Ripe

The read-head hummed it softly. "It's a winner, Dom" she exclaimed, "so sad and beautiful!" "Yes" said Scarlatti "It needs a lyric, of course, but who could sing it? It needs a very special kind of singing. In fact, there's only one woman who could do that number justice . . ." The girl nodded slowly. "You mean . . ." "Yes" said the composer sadly, and tore the manuscript into small pieces. You see, they were both thinking of Ma Rainey. It was rotten luck, it being only 1725, but Scarlatti had a wonderful sense of humour, and he saw the funny side afterwards.

Blues Takes A Hold

The blues lay more or less submerged until it came to the surface again in the region of the Missisippi at the end of the nineteenth century. They had a lot of trouble around there, what with the river refusing to stay away from their door,bad gin, and the saloons being raided all the time, and pretty well everyone had the blues. But the music was really made to *live* by such unhappy Welsh exiles as Bessie Smith, Ma Rainey and Big Joe Turner.

Its Peculiar Style

They used to be accompanied by the boogie-woogie pianists, which is why they acquired that peculiar style. They had to fit the song into the four or five chords that the pianist was stuck with. Often enough they hadn't the faintest idea what the man was playing, and they had to sort of *slide* their voice to meet the next note as it came. It was an Art. What

They all had one fault

came out was a fairly melancholy noise, which was just as well as that was the whole idea, anyway.

Most of the blues took the form of a lover's lament, just like Daffydd Gryffyth's, the theme being that the singer's man (or woman) had done left them ("Baby, Won't You Please Come Home?" "Empty Bed Blues" and so on). They were very sincere, these singers, for the simple reason that their men (women) *were* always leaving them. By the minute. It's easy enough to see why. Though all these singers, particularly the women, were extremely nice people—friendly, generous, warm-hearted—they all had one fault. They were awfully fat. And if there's one thing that makes a man feel small, it's a big woman; he sort of feels *overshadowed*.

Singers' Obsession With Own Ailments

It was hard lines on big girls, but no matter how much they shook, rattled, or rolled, they just couldn't lose weight. They got so obsessed with the idea that it began to creep into the blues ("It Must be Jelly 'Cos Jam Don't Shake Like That", "Scrap Your Fat", etc.). In the same way, the men blues singers drifted away from the Empty-Bed theme, and began moaning about their real or imagined ailments, such as indigestion. This kind of song had a very wide appeal, because there are so many sufferers from indigestion; and it was only natural that they came to regard the singer Leadbelly as their champion.

Understanding *The Blues: An Exercise*

The blues can consist of 12, 24 or 32 bars, but it must have a certain *form*, or *pattern*. It's very difficult to explain in musical terms, especially at this time of the year, and the best way to illustrate this pattern is to compare it to walking round a chair (don't ask me why—all I know is that this is the Done Thing). Perhaps you would care to try this simple exercise:

1. Walk round a chair *clockwise:* this represents the first 4 bars.
2. Walk round *anti-clockwise:* (the second 4 bars).
3. Now stand back and make some observations on the chair. (the last 4 bars).

Fun, isn't it?

I shall now do the same thing, this time letting my thoughts wander as I do. Let's see if we can really get into the *spirit* of the blues, if you see what I mean.

Stage	*Thoughts*
Clockwise: first 4 bars:	Here we go round the mulberry bush, no, chair, silly—why chair, though? Could be plant-pot, elephant, wellington boot . . .
Anti-clockwise: Next 4 bars:	Whirl around, start again, suppose someone comes in and sees me, right fool I'd look, what the hell am I doing this for anyway?
Standing back: last 4 bars:	Chair, uh, huh, wood, trees, can't see wood for, meant to be satin, ha, ha, four legs, just like cow . . .

Inspiration From Exercise

Time's up. I admit it all looks a bit confused as it is, but it only needs a little working on. I've already got my blues' titles, any way—"Ole Mulberry Bush", "Plant-Pot Blues", "Whirlaround Drag", "Cow-Chair Boogie" . . . oh, and heaps more.

Anyone Can Do It If They Want

Perhaps you'd like to try it? Off you go, clockwise first, and don't forget to let your thoughts wander. Now anti-clockwise, that's it. Now stand right back—oh, you've barked your shin! Naughty chair! Oh, what a fine flow of language . . . yes, I imagine that you've got the spirit of the blues, right enough.

In fact, if you don't mind my saying so, you're real gone, Man . . .

11

How to reach the Top of the Pops

Difficulty Of Being Simple

THE KEYNOTE of the popular song of today is, as everyone knows, *simplicity*. The words must be simple, the tune must be simple, and—let's face it—it must be designed to appeal to people who are simple. The trouble is, the simplicity business ends there, because the most important part—the actual writing of the thing—is not simple at all. It is very difficult. For normal people, in fact, it is well-nigh impossible.

Words And Music

Songwriters are always being asked, What comes first—the words or the music? Now the traditional way of going about it is, of course, is to choose some poem, preferably one telling a story, and weave a melody around it. Such poems are, unfortunately, hard to come by nowadays, though in Shakespeare's time you could buy them at ninepence a dozen with a Jew's Harp thrown in.

Time And Length Considerations

Falling back on such old works is, however, fraught with complications; there's the time element for a start. Anyone who tries setting the Iliad to music will have his work cut out, and even if he manages to finish it he'll have a job marketing it. It'd be a bit long even for an L.P. record. (I suppose he *could* try having it serialized on the T.V. He could call it "An Everyday Story of Country Folk" or something like that.)

Music And Words

Exactly the same kind of difficulties arise when you work the other way round—i.e., putting words to well-known music. How many people have ever succeeded in setting lyrics to any of the big symphonies, for example? Very few, I understand. "Ah, but what about Beethoven's Fifth?" someone will ask (there's always some bonehead who'll ask questions like this). Beethoven's Fifth is, admittedly, an exception to the rule, but then it doesn't actually have *words* to it—only the Morse code (. . . — and so on). But you can't say that it ever *really* caught on, the reason being that people who can sing in Morse don't grow on trees. (Though come to think of it, maybe they *do* grow on trees. Certainly none of them live in our street.)

What The Creative Artist's Work Emerges As

To which of these methods does the modern song-writer subscribe, then? The answer is, *neither*. If you buy him a drink he will unburden his sensitive soul; he will tell you, for instance, that far from being separated into words and music, his work emerges as a *homogeneous whole*. At least, that's what he'd say if he knew what a homogeneous whole was. The truth is, words of more than one syllable don't come easy to him—but then, isn't that always the way with genius? What he will try to put over to you is the idea that a good song grows *naturally*. Like a carbuncle.

A Typical Song-Writer At Work

Picture him at work now, in his attic room in Tin Pan Alley. On top of the piano lies a filled ash-tray, on the couch an empty blonde. On the piano stool, hopefully strumming the keys, slumps Paddy Z. Rosenberg (that's only a pseudonym, of course—there's no "Z" in his real name). As he strums, one note, one particular note, suddenly strikes him as being a particularly nice one. He says as much to the blonde, who

Picture him now in his attic room

looks doubtful. He plays it again, and it seems to hang triumphant in the air, towering above all the others.

Starting A Song

Let us suppose that this note is DOH. Right, says Mr. Rosenberg, now inspired, that's the note I'm going to use for the opening of my new number. Having done this, he now makes a shrewd decision; he decides that now is the time before the thing gets too complicated, to choose a word to go with DOH (he's no fool). It might be "I" or then again "You". He knows that both of these are excellent song-starters, as they give him such an awful lot of scope.

Building A Song

Next comes a note which, though possibly not up to the standard of DOH, is fairly pleasing all the same. This has to be either higher or lower than DOH, otherwise you will get what is known as *monotony;* and to go with it Mr.

Rosenberg selects a verb (he is very finicky about having the grammar just so). This might be "live", or "love", or "die". Now if the last note was *upscale*, the next one must be down, and vice-versa, and it will very likely be represented by a preposition. Let's say "in"—an excellent preposition with a character all its own. Upscale again for the definite article, followed by a noun; a big, two-syllable job this time, to add variety and sparkle. It could be "garden" or "ocean" or "station".

Scope For Lyrics

You see how easy it becomes when you apply Mr. Rosenberg's system. Already we have the first line of our song, with a catchy tune to match, So far we have

I/YOU LIVE/LOVE/DIE IN THE GARDEN/
OCEAN/STATION

You can please yourself which permutation you use. "You Die in the Ocean" has distinct possibilities, and you've got all kinds of ready-made rhymes like "devotion", "emotion" and "shaving-lotion". Personally I prefer "I Live in the Station" because the idea has a touch of real pathos about it.

You are now ready to proceed with your second line, and if you carry on with this method, who knows—you may have a smash-hit on your hands.

"I Live in the Station"—can't you just see it being splashed across the disc-sleeves? Can't you hear it stopping the show on Broadway? Can't you hear it being whistled in every works canteen?

What's that—you *can't*? Well—it seems that some people have *no* imagination . . .

WHAT MAKES A SMASH HIT?

Former Ways Of Song-Selling

THERE WAS a time when, having turned out a song, the procedure was for the writer to persuade some publisher to print as many copies as possible, then keep his fingers crossed while he waited to see how many people bought them. A hit that sold a hundred thousand copies was reckoned to be twice as successful as one that only sold fifty thousand . . . it was as easy as that. Life was much simpler in those days. If a song failed to come up to the publisher's expectations, there were two ways of "plugging" it:

1. Salesmanship

Singing salesmen were employed to go around the holiday resorts; they would warble their wares along the promenades, then everyone would rush to buy the song of their choice. Singing salesmen were very mobile. They had to be—as the catchy songs they sang had nothing whatever to do with the sheets they sold.

2. Advertising

When it seemed that a song had the hallmarks of a winner, but was a bit on the highbrow side, they used to publish it in the Sunday papers. It was very cunningly inserted between the fashion competition page and the sporting section, so that most of the family found themselves staring at it quite a lot. Even the subtlest of ballads was bound to make *some* kind of impression, and as often as not Father would surprise everyone, including himself, by crooning "Your Tender Smile Means all the World to Me" (Valse) while shaving on Monday morning. Highbrow songs like that wouldn't stand a chance nowadays.

Ukelele: Its Influence And Significance

The coming of the ukelele had a drastic effect on popular tunes, because people found that numbers like "Your Tender Smile Means All the World to Me" were pretty well un-strummable. They wanted tunes with only two or three chords, starting with C Major, and because very few could read music, they wanted diagrams to show them where to put their fingers. That accounts for those little squares with dots on them that used to appear on sheet music (someone once tried making diagrams for pianists, but there are eighty-five notes on the piano, and he found that "Home on the

Range" took a hundred-and-seventy-three pages).

Influence Of The "Talkies"

Everyone was glad when the "talkies" arrived and put the musical film on the map. The publishers didn't bother with the Sunday papers any more; they started putting colourful blurbs on the music-covers. Underneath a picture of Al Jolson it would have the caption: "As sung by Gracie Fields in 'Hell's Angels'". The popularity of the piece would then depend on the number of people who were enthusiastic about (a) Al Jolson, (b) Gracie Fields, and (c) "Hell's Angels". This was a bit rough on the writers of songs which never got all this publicity, and often enough they merely gathered dust in shop-windows (I refer to the songs, not the writers. I don't know, though . . .).

Function Of Gramophone Record

The greatest factor in the making of a smash-hit today, however, is the gramophone record. Here again there have been some big changes. At one time practically all records of popular songs were made by a man called Eustace Pottinger (Baritone: With Piano Accomp.). Occasionally it might say on the label "Arthur Merryweather (Tenor: With Piano Accomp.") but really it was this chap Pottinger all the time. (As a matter of fact he often played the Piano Accomp. and stuck the labels on himself.) He probably made an awful lot of money, but he must have suffered greatly from tonsillitis and schizophrenia. It makes you wonder if it was all worth it.

Overcrowding At Studios

Today, one-man acts like Pottinger are out of favour with gramophone people. They've had their duettists (Layton and Johnstone), trios (the Boswell Sisters), quartets (the Mills Brothers) but they never seem to be satisfied. They believe there's safety in numbers, and they won't start recording a popular song until they've assembled a clutch of engineers, three "echo-chamber" consultants, an augmented symphony orchestra, a celestial choir, a smaller vocal group, a claque of highly-skilled hand-clappers, an electronic organ, a few hand-picked instrumentalists to "back-up" the vocalist, and

. . . now who else was there? Oh, yes—the vocalist. When you also take into account the woman who goes round with the tea, it all adds up to a fair number of people. So much so, that the directors of one of the larger recording companies is beginning to worry about the accommodation problem. They also have nightmares that the day will come when the number of artists required to make a given record (X) is in excess of the number of people who buy it (X—1).

Disc-Jockeys A Rum Lot

Those who have the greatest influence in the sphere of gramophone records are the *disc-jockeys* (records, of course, are also called "discs", but you can't very well say "sphere of discs"—it sounds daft). The number of requests that reach the radio studios weekly is extraordinary, although they are not as numerous as they were. Not long ago, a certain disc-jockey played the same record in his programme three times, and did this six times in a week; which made the radio authorities scratch their heads. When they discovered the same man had composed the song and also sang it, they looked at one another and wondered if this was all right. It wasn't of course, and in the inquiry that followed a lot of funny things came out.

New Precautions

Not the least of these was the fact that over a million requests a month were arriving regularly from the Shetland Isles. As Lord Chemwell, the radio chief, shrewdly observed: "I doubt if there are that many people living in the Shetland Isles". He was right as usual. Agents employed by people like Paddy Z. Rosenberg had been posing as mothers of triplets in Aberdeen and octogenarians in Cardiff for too long. Now, things are very different, and stringent precautions are taken with all requests received at the studios (finger-print powder, bloodhounds, etc.).

Sight Before Sound?

Once more the song that reaches the Top of the Pops does so on its own merits. The snag is, that the making of a record gets more and more expensive. Sales psychologists have made the amazing discovery that there are millions of people who buy a record not for what it *sounds* like, but for what it *looks* like; and companies are vying with each other in seeking out the services of brilliant artists and writers to fill the space on their record-covers, or "sleeves". The illustrations are imaginative; a selection from "Porgy and Bess' will be illustrated by a girl in a low-cut dress; "Eine Kleine Nachtmusik" by a girl in a low-cut dress; "Haydn's 'Surprise' Symphony" by a girl . . . and so on. An album of Louis Armstrong favourites might well be surrounded by a sleeve-ful of off-the-cuff verses from Ezra Pound. In fact, some people are complaining that when they buy a record they don't know whether to hang it on the wall or put it in the book-case. They could, of course, try it on the gramophone . . .

12

The Backward Person's Dictionary of Musical Terms

ABANDONNE — Abandoned. E.g., Schubert's "Unfinished Symphony".

ABDAMPFEN — To "damp-off". Sometimes, especially during pieces like "The Ride of the Valkyries", the brass instruments tend to get overheated. And they haven't got an air-cooling system, either.

ACCIDENTAL — An F Sharp suddenly appearing in an easy piano piece is an *accidental*. It means you have to move up on to the black notes, which is serious. Accidental? More like some smart-alec's idea of a joke.

ADAGIO — At ease. Most players are careful about this order, because no sooner have they taken off their jackets than the conductor yells " 'Shun!".

AIR — A component of the bagpipe.

ANON. — An extremely prolific composer, now dead (if not, he must be past his best). He wrote "Green Grow The Rushes, O" and other things that no-one else will own up to.

BAGATELLE — Not worth playing.

BALLAD — A story-song. There are three kinds: 1. Stop - me - if - you've - heard - this - before; 2. Drawing-room; and 3. Plain dirty.

BALLADE — Ballad sung by a woman.

BARCAROLLE — Sort of Italian hot-dog.

BEN MARCATO — As I recall, he used to run a mandoline band in Birmingham about twenty-five years ago. I can't think how *he* got in here.

BOUCHE FERMEE — Mouth Closed. A typical piece of French exhibitionism, rarely seen nowadays. The number of singers who can make the music come out of their ears is rapidly dwindling.

CAMMINANDO — Walking. If you see a musician get up in the middle of a symphony and start down the aisle, then his music probably said *camminando*. (If not, then he ought to have asked if he could leave the room.)

COLORATURA — *Coloured* music. E.g., the Blues, "All God's Chillun", etc.

Coll' Arco Otherwise "With the Bow". An aria from the opera "Cock Robin".

Concert Pitch Site selected by a street musician.

Con Fuoco With fire. Be a good scout and rub a couple of wood-winds together.

Dehors Outside! Between you and me, there are certain songs which you daren't sing indoors. That is, unless you happen to be at a West End cabaret.

Demi Jeu Half-play to the French; half-time to you. If the drummer's doing nothing, he could start slicing the lemons on his timpani.

Eisteddfod A session presided over by a Gorsedd Beirdd Ynys Prydain, where they choose an Offydd and a Pencerdd, and where they often have a Cymanfa Ganu. (I think that clears *that* up.)

Elan Dash! The composer has here made a mistake.

Folk-Music The music of the *people*, usually performed before an audience of about six.

fp Loud and soft. You press *both* feet down on the piano pedals. Not to be confused with pf (soft and loud) which is a different thing altogether.

Gehalten Well held! Term of praise for a soprano who hangs on to a top note for a very long time. (When she lets go, some people follow up with OWZAT, from the Australian.)

HARMONY — A discordant type of singing heard outside public-houses.

HELL — Oh, dear! Another mistake.

INDECISO — Undecided. There are some bits that the composer doesn't know how to finish, and it's obviously a case of every man for himself.

LOCO — Like a man gone mad.

MEZZO PIANO — Half-soft: see LOCO.

NOCTURNE — A night-piece. E.g., George Sand.

pf — cf. fp.

OUVREZ — Well, it's no use trying to play the piano with the lid down, is it?

PIZZICATO — Pinched. The composer is actually admitting that this bit is not entirely original.

REEL — A slow movement between bars. After the Scotch.

RUBATO — Stolen. A more obvious snatch than a *pizzicato* piece.

SEC — Dry! Time you drained out your euphonium.

SGAMBATO — Walked off one's legs. The result of too much *camminando* (see ZURÜCK.)

SCHWELLWERK — Nice work!

SO BALD? — So soon? A rap on the knuckles for the pianist who tries to do Chopin's "Minute Waltz" in fifty seconds.

Tarantella This comes from Italy, where they have a giant spider called the Tarantula. Whenever one of these spiders gets bitten by a peasant, it goes into a sort of fit, called the *tarantella*. This kind of thing will always happen while peasants go around biting spiders.

Tonic Solfa A pick-me-up for singers, taken in the form of sol-fa tablets.

Torch Song A form of Light music that's gone out.

Volti Subito Turn round suddenly. The effect is rather pretty when a whole symphony orchestra does it together.

Zurück Back again. Cue for the man who's been *camminando* all this time.